Contents

Acknowledgments

A number of people contributed greatly to this project and deserve both mention and credit. Topping the list is Ben Avechuco of Techie's Alternative in Tempe, Arizona. Besides owning his own budding video production company, Ben is technical director of a local television station, where one of his responsibilities is training new employees. Ben's special expertise kept us all on track throughout the project, and many of the professional tips you will learn here come directly from him as do many of the photographs. It was Ben's influence that got me involved in video in the first place—he took the very first videos of my baby son.

Others who contributed their time and talents are Scott and Terri Drudge, Russell ("Bringemcrackem") VanSickle, Bruce Markham, Alan Lea, Tom Emerson, and Wiley the Wonder Dog. Maureen Megan Kane developed the concepts for the illustrations.

A number of equipment manufacturers took an active part. Most helpful in this group were Greg Smith of Ambico, Judy Fleming of RCA and Betty Spears of Kartes Video Communications. Thanks to one and all, even where specific names aren't mentioned.

The list wouldn't be complete without mention of Daniel (Danny Boy) and Cindy Williams—the centers of my life and the subjects for hours upon hours of my own home videos. Both put up with having cameras and lights aimed at them endlessly—and with long absences while I hid in the darkroom or in front of the keyboard and editing equipment.

CHILTON'S Guide
to
Using and Maintaining
Home Video Cameras and
Equipment

Introduction

Twenty years ago, the first home video deck was made available to the consumer. It weighed close to 80 pounds, took huge reels of inch-wide tape for just a few minutes of black-and-white recording, and cost about $6000. The camera for it cost just as much. Both were well known for breaking down often.

A decade later, video tape recorders weighed only about 50 pounds, could handle color, and cost about $2500. Now about half of the households in our country have VCRs. Expensive reels of tape have been replaced by inexpensive cassettes. Quality of reproduction and reliability of the machines have both gone way up, while the cost has dropped to the point that you don't have to look very hard to find a VCR for under $300.

As this revolution took place, another was dying: home movies. During the 1970s, the number of 8mm and Super 8 cameras skyrocketed. With the addition of a tiny strip of magnetic tape, sound was made possible. The greatest problem was cost. And with the soaring price of silver, that cost became even worse. A Super 8 cartridge holding just slightly over 3 minutes of silence now costs about $6. Processing the film will run about $2 more. To get an hour of film—again silent—you'll end up spending at least $160. To equal what can be squeezed onto a single video cassette, you'd pay more like $960.

Want a copy? There goes another $160 (probably more) per hour. With video you can make as many copies as you wish for the cost of the video cassettes.

Want sound? With film, that will drive the cost up at least half again. The sound automatically comes with video, although you *can* cut it off if you wish. Or if you prefer, you can easily replace existing sound with other sound.

Want portability? Forget it! The film camera is portable, but it's a little difficult to lug around the projector and screen. With the video camera, even if the viewer(s) don't have a video deck, they probably have a TV. Most camcorders can be hooked to the television for playback. No projector is needed. The financial advantages of video over film become quickly obvious (see table).

FILM/VIDEO COST COMPARISON

	Film	*Video*
Initial cost	$350	$1000
Media	160/hour	1/hour
Cost for first 6 hours	1310	1006
Cost for next 6 hours	960	6
Cost first 12 hours	2270	1012

There are other advantages, as well. With video there is no waiting for the processed film to come back. Editing tape is much easier than editing film. And, if you don't like what you've shot, with video tape you can back up and start again. Is it any wonder that video cameras have started to take over?

Although video is less expensive than film in the long run, it represents a hefty initial investment. You can find video cameras for less than $500 and camcorders for less than $1000. However, it's easy to spend two, three, or four times that and still be in the realm of "home" equipment.

Then come all the possible peripherals. You can buy wireless remote microphones. There are titlers, enhancers, editors, time/base coordinators—each of which can cost as much as a camera. Some will cost considerably more.

And there are so many choices to make. Which camera to get? Or maybe you should buy a camcorder—camera and recorder all in one. But again, which one? What do all those terms (E/V, A/V, autowhite, etc.) mean?

It helps to have some idea of how all this equipment works. Chapter 1 will tell you, in simple terms, how it functions. Having that basic understanding of what the equipment does, and how it does it, will help in effective operation. It will also help you to keep that expensive equipment alive and healthy over the years.

Chapter 2 details the various features and functions to look for when buying cameras, camcorders, and VCRs, including the different kinds of video imagers used inside to capture the picture on tape. Also covered are the various formats available. (There are presently four—

five if you count the miniaturized VHS-C, and six if you also count the newer SVHS.)

Chapter 3 discusses peripherals: both those you will find handy, and some that are a waste of money. Included are such things as lights, external audio equipment, signal enhancers, switchers, and editors.

The most delicate part of a video system is the tape. Chapter 4 tells you everything you need to know about the video tape, from buying it to storing it to taking care of it. You'll even learn how to make repairs to damaged tapes, thus rescuing your valuable recordings.

It has been said, very accurately, that a professional with a cheap camera will get considerably better results than an amateur who has the best equipment. Proper selection of equipment, and the quality of that equipment, is important. Proper operation is even more important. Chapter 5 shows you how to use your equipment to best advantage, along with some of the "tricks of the trade."

Photography of any kind is nothing more than capturing and recording light. An extreme example would be trying to take a picture in a black room – no light at all means no photograph (or, in this case, no videograph). Many people stop there, with the idea that all they really need is to blast the scene with plenty of light and everything is going to be fine. Chapter 6 will show you how false this is, and what you can do to make your home movies look professional.

Another aspect is planning. This might be as simple as having a rough idea of what is wanted, or it can be as complex as developing a complete storyboard. Chapter 7 deals with this important topic. Chapter 8 covers editing. Planning is certainly a part of this, since it allows you to do "in-camera editing," but there will be many times when other editing will be needed to change a nearly meaningless hodge-podge into something you'll be proud to show.

A growing number of people are putting special effects into their movies. These may be done as simply as using a different camera angle, or you can create effects that will rival Hollywood's. Chapter 9 shows how, but concentrates on simple, inexpensive ways to "spice up" your home video.

Equipment maintenance and troubleshooting is covered in Chapter 10; alone, it can save you many times the cost of this book. A dead camera can't make videos for you, but it sure can deplete your wallet. This chapter will tell you how to reduce the number of times you have to shell out money for technical services (or new equipment).

To help you over the terminology hurdle, a comprehensive glossary is included at the end of the book.

It's all here – from buying the equipment and operating it to best advantage, to making sure that it continues to operate, to dealing with a technician if you need that service. And right back to buying more equipment, should that day come.

Chapter 1

Home Video Equipment: How it Works

A basic understanding of how something works makes it easier to operate and often increases the lifespan of that equipment. It doesn't matter whether or not you can get inside a video camera to repair it. It matters even less if you could design that camera from spare parts.

Long ago it was known that light causes certain chemical reactions. This developed into the field of photography in the last century, when methods of causing *controlled* reactions were found. Before long, the chemicals were improved so that they could be coated onto flexible plastic; the process was inexpensive enough that everyone could take home snapshots. The field continued to advance and improve. Early in this century, motion pictures were made possible. Then came movies with sound. Then movies in full color. Then home movies. Then home movies in color. Then home movies in color and with sound.

The movies themselves were (and are) based on a chemical reaction. The sound for home movies was recorded magnetically.

There are many similarities between film photography and video photography. There are also many differences. Light strikes film and causes a photochemical reaction, and that's it. If you want more sensitivity (film speed) or want a b&w image, you use a different film. There is no such thing as a video tape more (or less) sensitive to light, nor is there such a thing as b&w video tape.

Videography also begins with a photochemical reaction, as the light strikes the pickup device (imager) and causes an electrical charge to develop. Sensitivity is determined by that imager, which then generates the signals. These signals are then processed electronically and recorded onto a magnetic tape (Fig. 1–1). Later, the magnetic

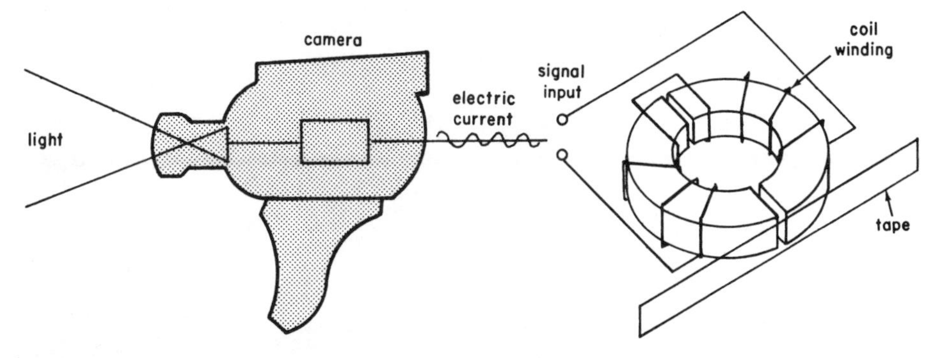

FIG. 1–1 Basic videography: Light strikes the pickup device, which creates an electrical charge. The charge generates a magnetic field in the recording heads, and impulses are stored on the video tape.

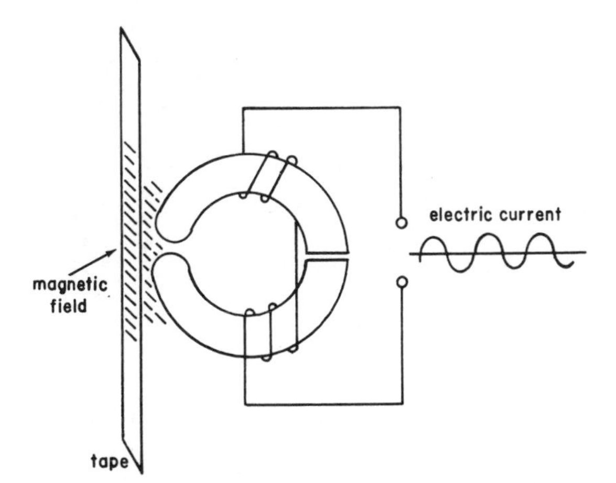

FIG. 1–2 In playback, the stored magnetic field stimulates electrical currents, which are processed and eventually end up on your television as sight and sound.

fields stored on the tape stimulate the signals that are processed electronically (again) for playback (Fig. 1–2).

PICKUP DEVICES (VIDEO IMAGERS)

Professional cameras use three pickup devices (also called video imagers)—one for each of the video primary colors (red, green and blue, often abbreviated RGB). Quite often the imagers are tubes, although photosensitive electronic chips are coming into more and more common use. (With both studio and home video cameras, the trend is to use a chip instead of a tube. The chip tends to be more sensitive, while simultaneously less prone to damage from too much light.)

With three tubes or chips instead of a single pickup, the resulting image in a professional video camera is clearer and truer in color. However, the professional camera also carries a hefty price tag.

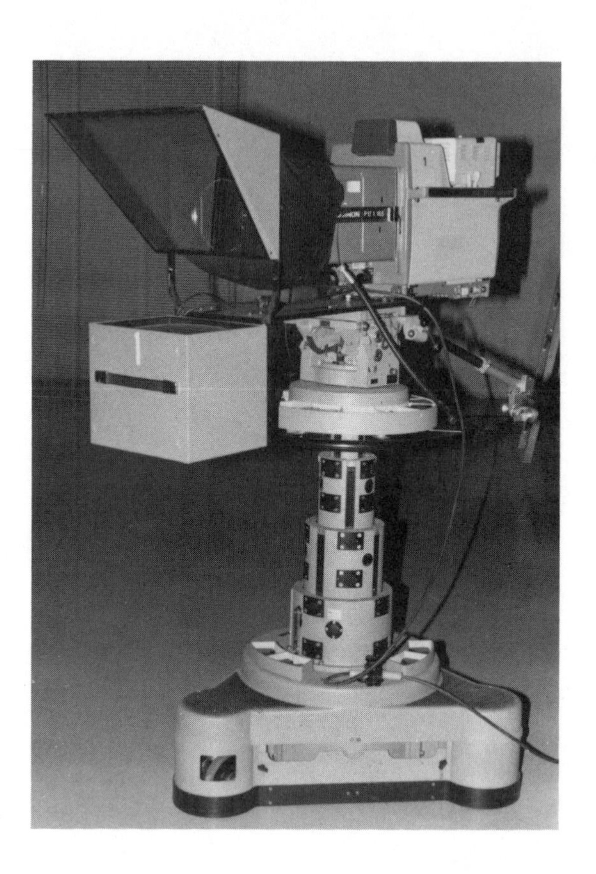

FIG. 1–3 A studio video camera.

A home video camera has a single device that converts light into electrical impulses. The photochemical reaction caused by light striking the pickup is converted into electricity, which can then cause the electromagnetic video head to store the image on tape.

The two most common in-home video cameras are Saticon and Newvicon. Professional cameras, and a few home cameras, also use a lead-based substance with the brand name of Plumbicon. The operational difference is minimal. All three work very well. The only real difference is in the chemical makeup. Some years ago Saticon was used in studio cameras, while Newvicon was used more in surveillance cameras. Although both have greatly improved and now are about equal, you might hear that Saticon has better color while Newvicon has better sensitivity to light. This may have been true once, but isn't now.

In short, it isn't critical which is used when you go out to buy a camera.

With a film camera, the light is let in and allowed to strike the surface of the film, where it sets off a photochemical reaction. The chemicals embedded on the film base change. Other chemical reactions from the developer make those changes more permanent. You end up with a negative or slide.

FIG. 1–4 A video pickup tube.

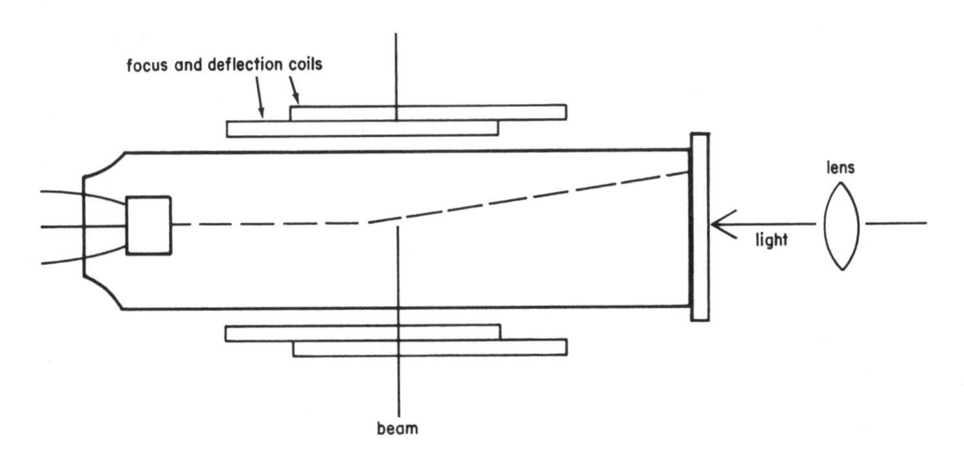

FIG. 1–5 Operation of a video pickup tube.

Filmed movies are exactly the same. In this case, the same process happens again and again, from frame to frame. Each frame is slightly different than the one before it. Show these in sequence and the illusion of motion returns.

A video camera is quite different, even while being very much the same. The pickup of the camera reacts chemically with the light that strikes it. Instead of becoming a permanent image, this kind of photochemical reaction creates a voltage. The electronic signals can then be processed by the circuits and recorded magnetically on tape.

In a tube camera, the function is somewhat like a television in reverse. Light strikes the photosensitive surface of the tube. This surface is electronically scanned, much like the screen of your television set is scanned when it "paints" the picture. One complete scan is called a *field*, with two fields making up a *frame*, and with each frame being somewhat (weakly) analogous to a frame on movie film. Play back those frames quickly in sequence and you have the illusion of motion.

The trend is away from tubes and toward something called CCD (charge coupled device) chips. Also coming into use, both in circuitry and in the pickups, is MOS (metal-oxide semiconductor). There are a number of reasons for this.

"Chip" cameras can be made smaller and lighter, since a chip is smaller and lighter than a tube. They also tend to require less power, which is wonderful for battery-operated equipment. This low power drain is especially true of MOS. Even more importantly, a chip is highly resistant to permanent damage from too much light. Aim a tube camera at a bright white surface for too long and it will "burn." This won't happen with a chip camera.

Another advantage is in a way a chip handles incoming light. The constant scanning of the tube (twice for each frame) in a tube camera can easily cause blurring if the subject or the camera is moving too quickly. But the surface of a chip is divided into about 200,000 light sensitive spots (called *pixels*, for picture elements). The light falling on these spots creates individual electrical charges, thus helping to reduce blurring. The chip "fills" and then dumps the entire collection to a "frame memory storage." The chip is then erased and begins all over again. With most chip cameras, this happens 30 times per second, which gives the video camera an effective shutter speed of $\frac{1}{30}$th of a second. (A tube camera scans the pickup surface in $\frac{1}{60}$th of a second, creating a *field*. Two fields are needed for one *frame*, which means that the tube camera also has an effective shutter speed of $\frac{1}{30}$th of a second for a complete frame.)

Compared to a film camera, this is somewhat slow and there is some blurring as a result. However, the way the video camera works

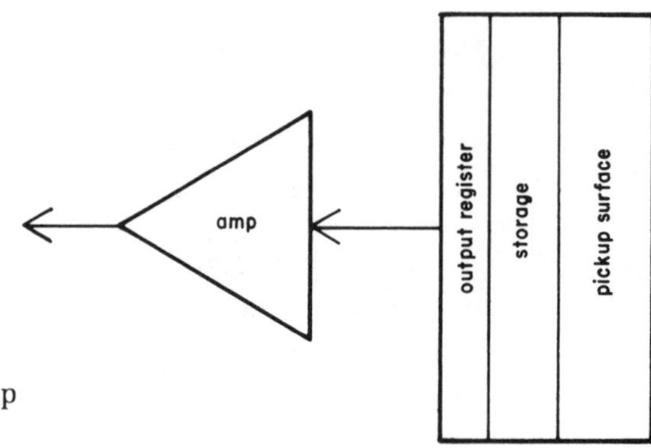

FIG. 1–6 How an electronic chip pickup works.

reduces the blurring that would normally result from slow shutter speed. Usually the blurring isn't seen except when the playback is paused. Some new cameras boast of having a "high speed shutter," which means that the circuits are specially designed so that the pickup fills and dumps faster—as fast as $^1/_{1800}$th of a second. Each frame is completed so quickly that blurring is almost nonexistent. For this to work, light intensity must be strong enough so that the image is quickly built up on the pickup. As with a film camera, a fast shutter speed requires either bright light or a wide aperture.

Whichever video camera you own, you can't set the shutter speed. You *can* set the iris (aperture) to allow more or less light in. With a video camera, the more intense the light, the more voltage is generated. Aim the camera into a very bright scene with the iris wide open and there will be so much signal generated that the end result will be washed out. With too little light, the image will be dim and colors askew.

A PRIMER ON COLOR

The three video primaries are red, green, and blue (Fig. 1–7). Don't confuse these with the color primaries of physics (red, yellow, and blue). The video circuits in the camera and in your television set handle colors in a slightly different manner.

Video red is, by nature, more intense, meaning that it has more of a tendency to "bleed" and blur. Yet it makes up only about 30% of the

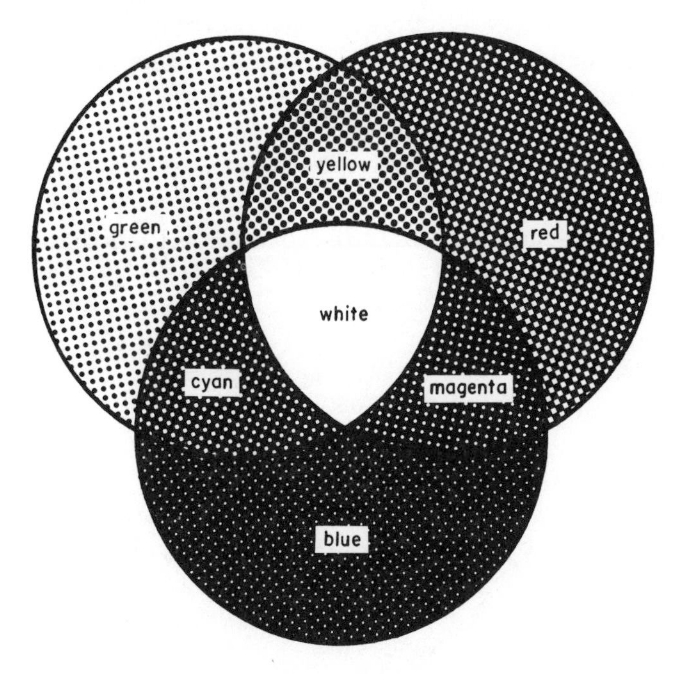

FIG. 1–7 Primaries on the video color wheel.

scene (and the camera is adjusted accordingly). Virtually all scenes are made up of 30% red, 59% green and 11% blue. As a consequence, in low light the reds and blues start to disappear, leaving a scene that has a green cast to it. Compensating circuits are built into the better video cameras, but they have limitations. Expect a scene to acquire a greenish, grainy appearance under low light conditions.

You may also notice that your reds aren't true, tending toward a red-orange; likewise, colors that include red in a blend might be off a little. This is a characteristic of video red, both in the camera and in the TV. Pay close attention when watching TV: unless you have an extremely high-quality monitor, you'll notice a slight miscoloring even in professional video taping. Most people are so used to seeing it that they don't notice until they buy their own camera and are purposely watching for color differences.

The exact sensitivity settings inside the camera are tuned either to sunlight or to standard incandescent photo floods (which are not *quite* the same as the incandescent lights in your home). Almost without exception, you'll get the best picture and colors when shooting outside. This is due largely to quantity of light available. Even sensitive cameras work best with more light. What is important is that the camera can be adjusted to the type of light being used.

Your eye doesn't usually see it, but each type of light source has a different color. When compared to sunlight as standard "white light," the incandescent lights in your home are red. A shadow outside is blue. The color of light is measured as a temperature in degrees Kelvin (see table). It has nothing at all to do with the actual physical heat of the source. (A photo flood rated at 3400°K isn't several thousand degrees hot.) It's all based on a perfect black body at absolute zero. Warm that black body to a certain temperature and it will give off a certain color of light. The hotter it gets, the more blue the light becomes until it eventually passes into the invisible ultraviolet range and beyond.

When using a film camera, the film is changed or the light is filtered, depending on the light being used. Film balanced for daylight will give a reddish image if used indoors without a filter. With a video

MEASURING THE COLOR OF LIGHT

Source	*Temperature (°K)*
Incandescent	2700–3600
Fluorescent	4500
Sunlight	5600
Shadows or clouds	6000–7000

camera, internal filtering is more commonly used; adjustment may be done with an automatic circuit or manually.

Most home video cameras have a single control for the adjustment. This is the *white balance*. The proper combination of the three primaries makes white. So, once the camera is set to record white under the given conditions, other colors should also be correct—or very close. It does depend somewhat on the white you use to balance the colors. If it's impure, the balance won't be quite accurate. The more inaccurate the white used, the more inaccurate the balance will be.

Many cameras are equipped to handle this automatically in one of several ways. The least expensive video cameras have a white balance button. Aim the camera at something white, push this button, and the camera's circuits read the incoming light and balance for that white. A full autowhite is similar to this electronically, but the function takes place constantly and by itself. As the camera picks up different incoming light, it constantly adjusts and readjusts.

All cameras have some kind of manual override—the simplest being a single slide or knob, the more complex ones providing a different adjustment for each video primary.

The only accurate way to set the camera manually is by connecting it to a color TV or monitor. Anything else is guesswork. Markings on the adjustment controls are only approximations, and even then are often inaccurate. If you're adjusting the camera manually, don't trust them.

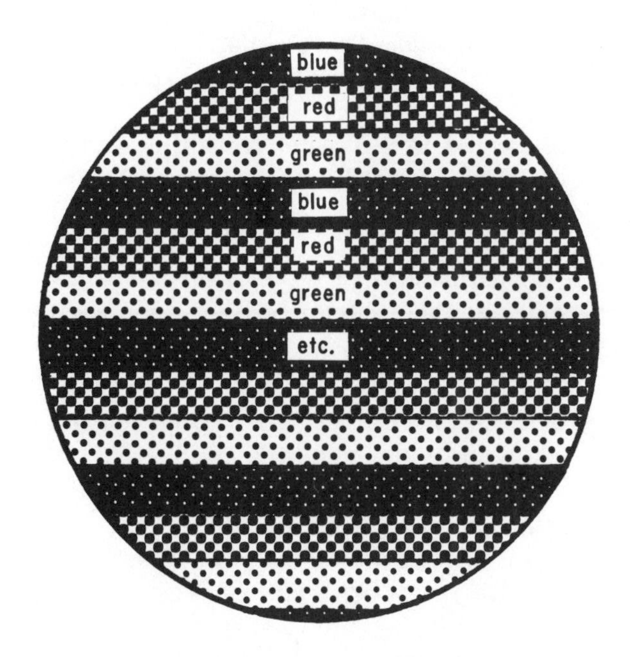

FIG. 1–8 A stripe filter controls the color of light.

RECORDING IMAGE AND SOUND

If you put AC (alternating current) through a coil of wire, a magnetic field is generated. Conversely, if you move a magnetic field by a coil of wire, the result is an electrical current. Vary the current, and the resulting field also varies. Vary the field, and the current varies as well.

Both audio and video recordings are based on this principle. The tape is a length of plastic (usually Mylar) with a coating of particles that can take and hold a magnetic field. The incoming audio and video signals are electrical currents. The audio and video recording heads are small electromagnets. The incoming current stimulates these. They in turn impress the magnetism onto the tape as it passes by.

Later, the same tape passes over the heads in the playback mode. Now the stored magnetic fields stimulate the coils in the heads and produce electrical pulses.

In both directions, the circuitry of the unit processes the electrical impulses. The incoming light and sound is changed to electrical signals, which in turn cause the recording heads to generate the magnetic field, which is then impressed onto the tape. Later, the magnetic field stored on the tape causes the playback heads to generate electrical pulses which are processed and turned back into the video and audio.

An audio signal is fairly uncomplicated and has a narrow range of frequencies. Accurate recording and playback are not difficult to accomplish. With many VCRs, it is recorded in a straight line (linear), just as it is with an audio cassette recorder. Video has a much broader range of frequencies, which makes it more difficult to record accurately, especially when color is involved.

You probably know that a faster recording and playback speed improves the sound of a recording. The same is true of video, only more so. While you can reproduce acceptable sound at less than 2″ per second, the tape speed needed to properly reproduce video (or high fidelity audio) is measured in feet per second.

The first video recorders did just this. Powerful motors were used to drag the tape across the recording heads at great speed. This caused some real problems. It takes time for the motors to get up to speed, and time for them to slow down. Operating speed caused strain on the tape. Friction throughout the machine was increased. Breakdowns were common.

To reduce problems—and cost—tape speed has been slowed down. To make up for the slower speed, the video heads were moved. VCRs and the recording/playback sections of camcorders have a video head assembly that spins at about 3600 rpm, even though tape speed is just slightly over 1″ per second even on "high speed." (Standard for VHS is just over 33mm/sec on two-hour play; about 11mm/sec on six-

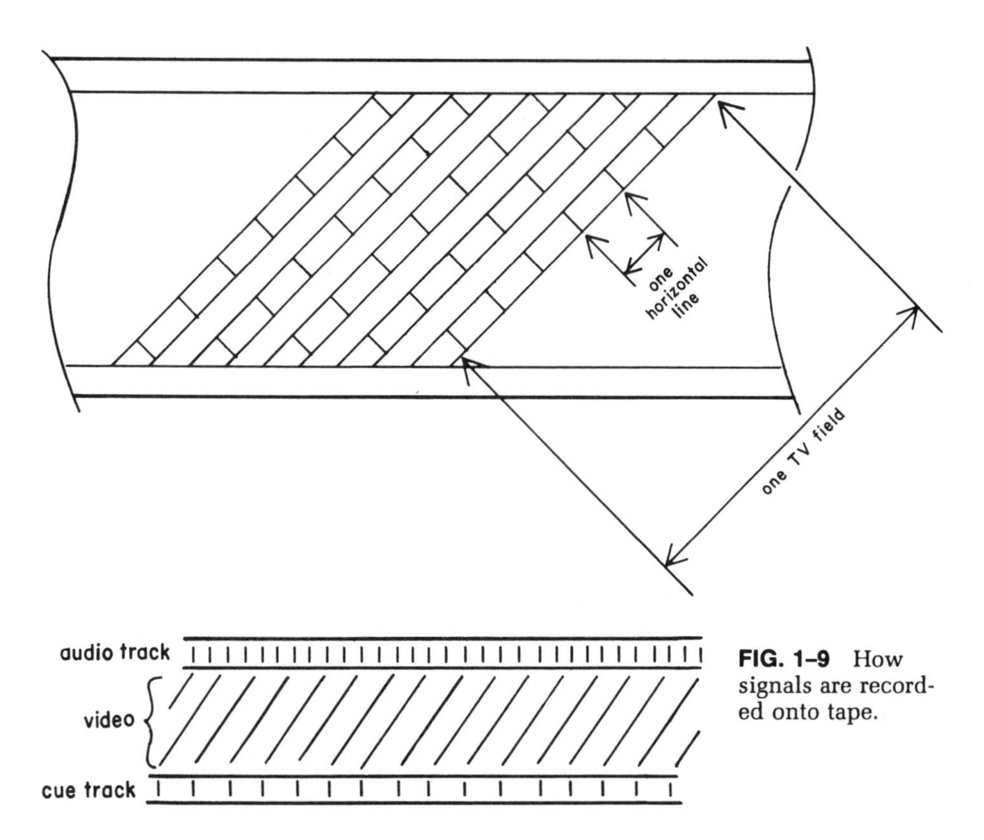

FIG. 1–9 How signals are recorded onto tape.

hour play. Multiply by .0394 to convert millimeters to inches, and you'll find that the tape is moving along at about 1⅓″ per second on fast speed, and at less than ½″ per second on long play.)

The spinning head assembly increases the *effective tape speed* to the point where as much as 8 hours of recording can be crammed into a $6 cassette that is 4″ × 7″ in size (instead of having 30 minutes on a $100 15″-wide reel).

To accomplish effective head speed while keeping actual tape speed down, a way was needed to "stack" the recording. This is accomplished by using a spiral (helical) motion of the tape across the heads. The video is recorded in streaks. As the tape moves forward, the video signals are placed onto the tape in hundreds of such streaks per inch (Fig. 1–9).

As the tape is inserted into the machine, a pin releases a catch along the side of the cartridge. The protective door at the front of the cartridge is then released and raised, thus exposing the tape. For *play* or *record,* pinch rollers grab the tape. Various pins, arms and guides then bring the tape into the machine and wrap it around the video head assembly. Its path across the head is angled because the video head assembly is tilted. As the video head spins, it crosses the tape diagonally.

This is how the video image is recorded and how it is played back

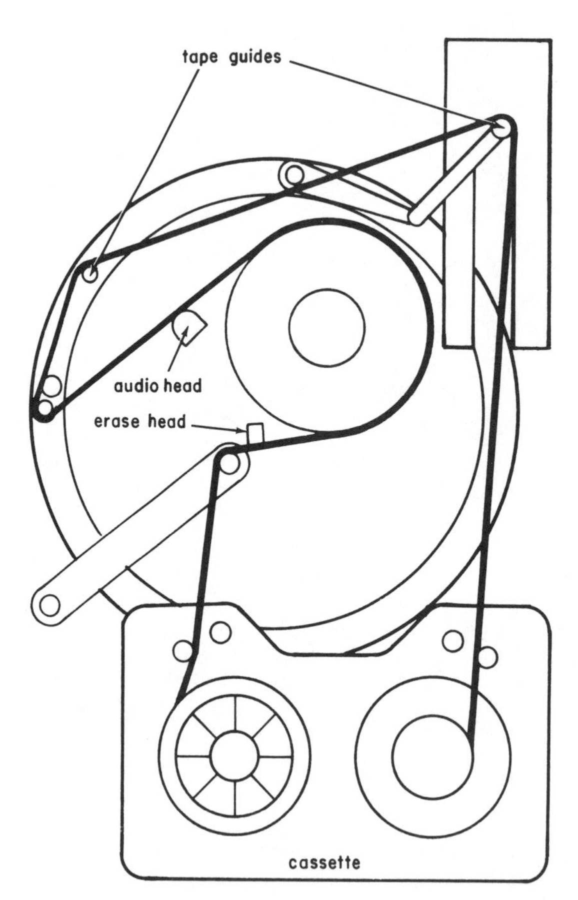

FIG. 1–10 Tape path through a VCR.

later. This is the helical scan of the VTR, with the tilt of the head assembly and angle of the tape being the azimuth. For everything to work correctly, all must be in proper alignment. The adjustment for this is critical. It's *not* the sort of thing you can do at home. Replacement of the head assembly demands alignment, which is why you can't handle that job, either.

In most VCRs, the tape first travels across an erase head, which is not active during playback. This theoretically clears the tape of any existing image and sound. Because there is a slight distance between where the video head is recording the image and where the erase head is removing the old image, a small amount of tape retains old video image. The result is a momentary glitch, as the old and new images are interfering with each other. During playback, you'll see momentary wiggly color lines on the screen. Once that tiny portion of tape has passed the video heads, the new image will be the only thing on the tape and the wiggly lines will disappear.

The only solutions are to either use virgin tape (tape that has never been used) or to use a machine that has a "flying erase head." In this case, the erase heads are mounted on the head assembly, right next to the video heads. This way, erasure of the old image takes place simultaneously with recording of the new image.

The audio head comes last. The sound is put on a linear track at the top of the tape. It's similar to the sound recorded on a standard audio cassette.

One more thing is needed. There has to be a way to coordinate all the various signals and parts both to the VTR itself and to the television or monitor that is displaying it. This is called synchronization.

At the bottom of the tape is the *control track*, also referred to as the *sync track* or *cue track*. The pulses on this track keep everything in pace, telling the VTR where to start and stop each field and frame (there are two fields to each frame) and how the audio is timed to the video.

All of this is done electromagnetically. The tape is a stream of Mylar (a DuPont brand name; the generic name is polyethylene terephthalate, or PET). The Mylar tape has a coating of metallic particles, usually a form of iron oxide, capable of being magnetized.

NOISE, OR SIGNAL DISTORTION

Briefly, the incoming light and sound are changed into electrical signals which generate a magnetic field in the record heads, which then affects the magnetic particles on the tape. Later, the tiny magnetic fields stored in the particles moves across the coils of the playback heads and generates the electrical signals that are changed back into a reproduction of the original video and audio. Unfortunately, while all this is happening, errors can creep in. The circuits themselves introduce distortion; the translation of signal to magnetism and back to signal isn't 100% perfect. Even the voltage that powers the unit contains imperfections.

All these unwanted signals are called *noise*. They get amplified right along with the signals that you do want. Under most circumstances, this isn't a serious problem. However, if the signal level is low, or if the signal-to-noise (S/N) ratio is poor, the recording and playback can be annoying or useless.

If you want to record a voice in a crowded room, and the voice is low in volume, the background noise will be relatively higher as a ratio to the wanted signal. If you boost amplification to pick up the voice, you also amplify all other voices and background noises.

The same is true of video. Shooting in low light introduces more video noise. Brighter light allows a better S/N ratio, but too much light can overload the camera, or permanently damage ("burn") a tube pickup. If the overload lasts, the pickup device will be burned all over, resulting in a degraded image (or no image). Chip-type pickups are not as prone to light level overload damage.

Chapter 2

Cameras, Camcorders, and VCRs

Before 1982, you had two choices. You could spend $30,000 on a professional camcorder; or you could easily plunk down $1000 for a home video camera, then buy a portable VCR so that you and the camera could wander around.

Then, in 1982, the first home camcorders hit the market, and the number of options increases steadily. Now you can go with Beta, VHS, VHS-C or 8mm. One company is developing a 4mm video tape that may become available in the near future. Exciting advances are being made in digital video recording.

The first video cameras demanded lighting equivalent to a bright, sunny day. Shooting inside with available light was unheard of. At the very least, photo floods were needed.

The first portables required a lot of battery power. Unless you bought a heavy, powerful (and expensive!) battery pack, you had little choice but to find a nearby AC outlet, which in turn meant carrying along a heavy-gauge extension cord, and even then limiting your range.

All that has changed.

You can still buy a video camera and VCR combination. Some claim that you get superior results this way; others disagree. Or you can opt for the convenience of a camcorder, with the camera and recorder together.

When you set out to choose your equipment, you'll face a lot of choices. The dealer's showroom seems to have a thousand cameras made by a hundred different companies. You may wonder if you'll ever understand all the terminology: as with so many technical fields, the world of video is full of terms and catch phrases.

"Yeah, you'll like this VidiPro 9000CXA. It's 11 lux, and a true 11 lux. That ½" Saticon imager is one of the best on the market. It has a

FIG. 2–1 A closeup of the controls on a typical video camera.

FIG. 2–2 This titler may seem complicated, but is actually quite straightforward to operate.

built-in character generator you can use for titling and can even genlock. It has complete A/V dub capability in and out, and of course a very nice E/V. Best of all, it has the most accurate automatic white balance you can buy at any price."

Don't worry; it's not at all hard to understand. There are just a few things you need to understand and compare, and we'll discuss those in the following sections. The manufacturers all produce decent quality merchandise, keeping in mind that you get what you pay for: don't expect a $600 camera to produce the same quality image as a $1200 camera (although it just might!).

TUBE VS. CHIP PICKUP DEVICES

As explained in Chapter 1, the heart of the video camera is the pickup device. This is an electronic module inside the camera that converts the light into electrical impulses.

Professional cameras use three pickup devices. If you hear of a three-tube camera, this is what is meant. There is a separate pickup device for each of the video primaries (red, green, and blue). Home cameras use a single pickup device. As a consequence, no matter how good a home camera is, it can't produce results like what you'd see from a professional studio. Don't expect it, because you won't get it. This doesn't mean that you won't get good results.

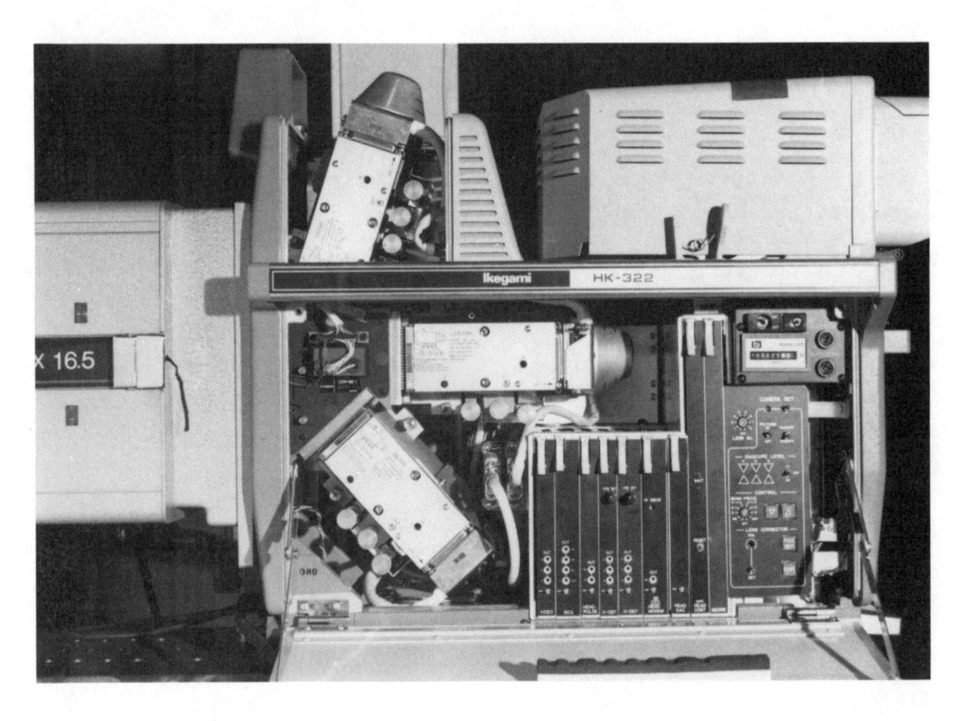

FIG. 2–3 Inside a studio video camera.

FIG. 2–4 A tube camcorder.

FIG. 2–5 One disadvantage of a tube camera is that bright light can burn the tube, leaving a permanent spot on the tube and on any taping you do. The tube burn shows here on the stable roof.

FIG. 2–6 A CCD camcorder, the Minolta Master Series-C3300. Photo courtesy of Minolta Corp.

FIG. 2–7 An MOS camcorder, the Minolta Movie CR-1200S AF. Photo courtesy of Minolta Corp.

The two most common types of pickup are Saticon and Newvicon. Either provides a good image, and the two are roughly equivalent; they are discussed in detail in Chapter 1. What matters a little more is size. Most home cameras use a single ½″ pickup. A few of the newer models have a ⅔″ pickup, which tends to be a bit more sensitive. It's also more expensive. Either will do a fine job. Testing the particular camera will let you know if the added cost is worth it.

There are two kinds of image pickup: tube and electronic chip. The tube is scanned in a manner similar to that of a television screen. The chip "fills up" as the incoming light affects the surface.

At the moment, video chip technology is still relatively new, which means that it generally costs more than tube technology. There will also be more complicated circuitry in the chip camera: for example, it will have a memory as a storage buffer between the pickup and the tape.

Both types work well. Most studios still use the tube-type, both because they are satisfied with the operation and because replacing it with newer technology is very expensive (to put it mildly). So, if you already have a tube camera, there is probably no reason to "upgrade." When it comes to buying a new home video camera, both have advantages and disadvantages.

The primary advantage of tube cameras is that they are usually less expensive for equivalent features. The main advantage of the chip camera is that the chip isn't as prone to damage. This is particularly true when it comes to burning. If the incoming light is too bright, a tube will be burned (insensitive). This may appear on your video as an area that is always a little lighter, or it could appear as a white spot (Fig. 2–5). If the light that caused the burn is uniform across the tube, the entire tube can be ruined.

It's possible to damage a chip if the incoming light is too bright, but this rarely happens. It *won't* happen under normal shooting conditions.

The most common *type* of chip is a charge-coupled device (CCD). RCA has come up with a new design that uses metal-oxide semiconductor (MOS) for the imager. Both produce fine results. Their characteristics are similar, but MOS circuits and components are used in camera specifications for high efficiency and low current drain. This in turn makes it possible to use a smaller battery, or to operate the camera for a longer period with a standard battery.

LUX, OR CAMERA SENSITIVITY

Sensitivity of a camera to light is rated in *lux*. The lower the number, the more sensitive the camera.

Lux is a metric measurement of light intensity. 1 lux is equivalent to the light from a candle spread evenly over a surface area of 1 square meter from a distance of 1 meter (see Fig. 6–1). That's not very bright. Your eye will have no trouble seeing it, but a camera won't be able to see it.

The light from a candle at a distance of 1 foot spread across a surface of 1 sq. ft. is 1 foot-candle. 1 foot-candle is equal to about 10 lux. A flashlight 3 feet away represents about 250 lux. A cloudy day is between 25,000 and 35,000 lux, depending on time of day. A bright and clear sky at noon is about 100,000 lux.

High-quality cameras today boast a rating of 7 lux, which is a bit exaggerated in virtually all cases. That 7 might more realistically be 9 or 10 lux—still very sensitive. A rating of 10 lux merely means that the camera can pick up an object in that low light; it *doesn't* mean that it's going to do a good job, or that there will be decent color. The image is likely to have a greenish cast and to be grainy.

Those low-light rated cameras still need 500 lux or more to create a decent image. Less sensitive cameras will require correspondingly more light before an acceptable image is produced. That extra sensitivity costs: a camera rated at 10 lux is going to cost more than one with a 100 lux rating. You'll have to decide for yourself if the extra sensitivity is worth the added cost. In most cases, it is, especially if you intend to do indoor taping.

OPTICAL AND ELECTRONIC VIEWFINDERS

There are two kinds of viewfinders for home video cameras: optical and electronic. Optical viewfinders are like those found on "regular" cameras. The least expensive is like a hole. You look through the hole and see approximately what the camera will pick up. Manual focusing is often a matter of guesswork. A step above this is a true rangefinder, where focusing the camera will also focus the image in the viewfinder.

The problem with either is something called *parallax*. This means that what you see and what the camera sees are slightly different. At a distance this isn't usually important. The closer you come to the object being photographed, the more severe the parallax error (Fig. 2–8). As an extreme example, if you put your finger directly in front of the lens, the camera will see and photograph it—but *you* won't be able to see your finger through the rangefinder.

Single lens reflex (SLR) is an optical method of viewing the scene through the lens. What you see and what the camera sees are the same, since you're looking through the lens from a system of mirrors. This is fairly easy to do with a film camera since the film camera uses a shutter to expose the film. You can see through the lens until that fraction of a second when the shutter moves. At this point, the reflex mirror moves out of the way so that the light can strike the film.

With a video camera, there is no shutter. The pickup device is in constant operation when the camera is running. Consequently, optical through-the-lens viewing with a video camera is extremely difficult to accomplish. It's easier, and cheaper, to design the camera to use an electronic viewfinder. This is one reason why SLR video cameras are rare.

An electronic viewfinder (E/V) is like a miniature b&w television set. As the light causes a reaction on the pickup device, it also stimu-

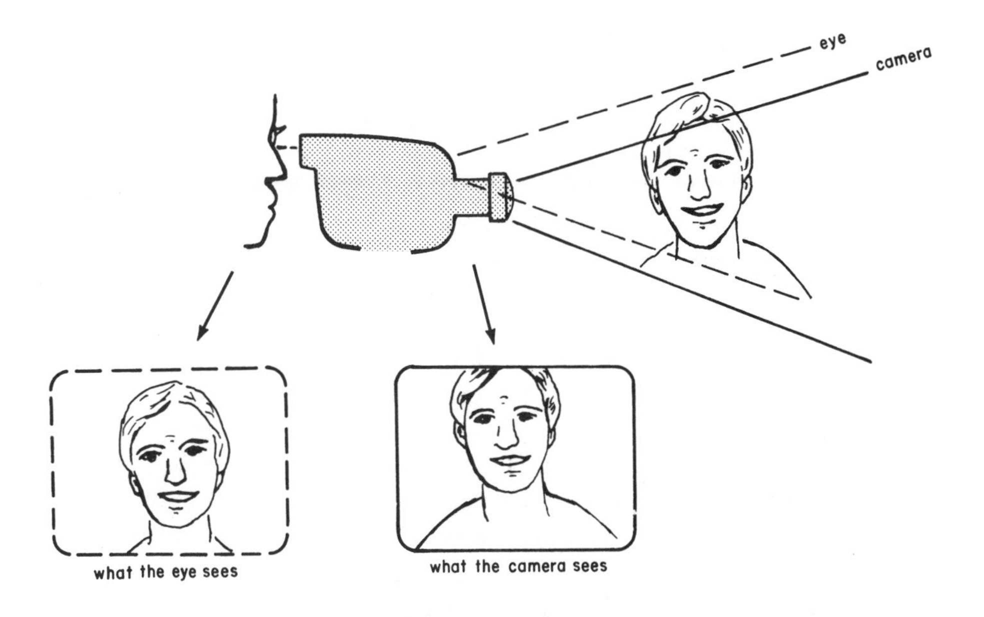

FIG. 2–8 Parallax: what you see and what the camera sees differ.

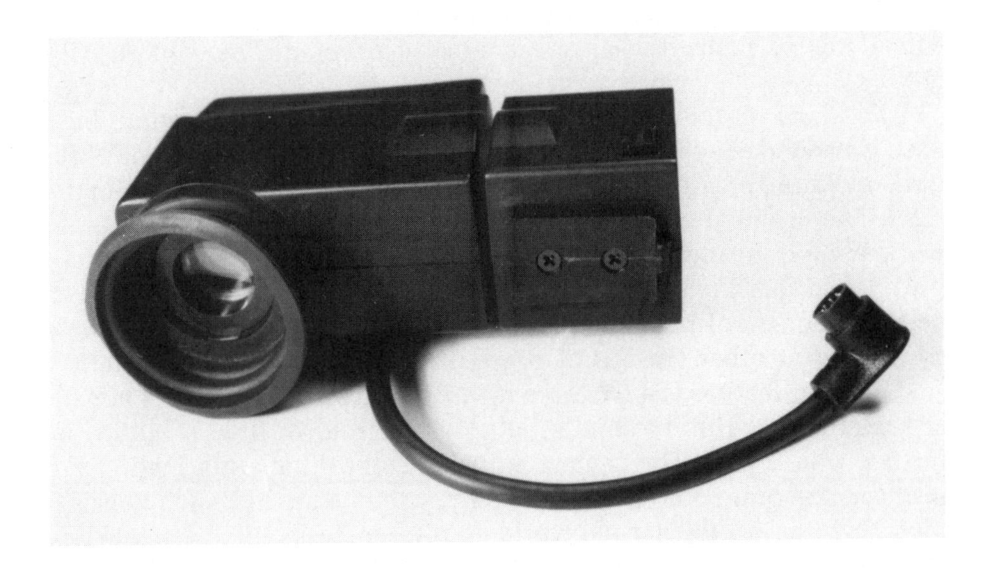

FIG. 2–9 An electronic viewfinder.

lates the signals used to drive the viewfinder. What it comes down to is that you see what the camera sees.

Obviously, a camera that uses an electronic viewfinder is going to be more expensive than one that has only a little hole. However, there are enough advantages to having such a viewfinder to warrant the cost. The most obvious advantage is that you see what the camera sees. You won't find out later that someone's head or some other important part of the scene has been cut off. Second, despite the lack of color in the viewfinder, you quickly learn how to set the camera controls for the best image by being able to see it as the camera does. Looking through an optical viewfinder reveals less, since your eye is then doing the seeing instead of the camera. A scene may look fine to your eye, but the electronic viewfinder will let you know that it's going to be very weak in the recording, or that parts of the scene are going to disappear. (Some professionals even prefer using a b&w viewfinder, since it reveals contrast levels so well.)

Third, most camcorders and many camera/recorder sets that have the E/V can also play back the image through that viewfinder. Some even have a "review" feature which allows you to look at the last few seconds automatically without having to switch over to the VTR function. This comes in very handy, especially for in-camera editing.

WHITE BALANCE AND THE COLOR OF LIGHT

Walk from outside into a lighted room. To your eye, everything will seem to be just fine. However, the color of the light has changed considerably. Your eye has automatically adapted. The camera will not.

To make the color correction for different lighting, a white balance is needed. The least expensive method is a manual control. With a wheel, knob, or slide, the operator can adjust the camera to available light. The problem is that such a manual adjustment is largely guesswork. Even if the manual control is marked for the different light qualities, those markings are approximations. To do the job right, you'll need a color monitor while making the adjustment. (A monitor is a good idea for other reasons also; we'll discuss some of them later.)

A better feature is a *lockable white balance*. The camera is aimed at something white under the lighting to be used, then a button is pushed (Fig. 2–10). The camera adjusts itself to that white, which in turn sets the other colors. For accuracy, you need to use a white card. Most "whites" in the normal world aren't. The less pure the white being used to set the camera, the more inaccurate the camera will be for colors.

A fairly recent feature that is being seen more and more is *auto white*. This feature causes the camera to automatically adjust itself to changing light qualities. The most common problem is one of inaccuracy, due to inherent problems with the circuits or because the camera adjustments are centered around an average. More important, even the most perfect auto white is easy to fool. Unusual lighting or mixed lighting can cause a problem (Fig. 2–11). So can a scene that is pre-

FIG. 2–10 Aiming the camera at a white card under the same light as the scene enables you to accurately set and lock the white balance.

FIG. 2–11 Light coming from different sources can confuse the auto white feature. Incandescent light, fluorescent light, and sunlight are all present in this scene. Each has a different color temperature.

dominantly one color. In such cases, it is best to switch to manual (see Chapter 5).

IRIS: A CAMERA'S EYE

As the amount of light increases or decreases, the pupil in your eye opens or closes accordingly. The muscle that controls this is the iris. In still photography, adjusting a camera for the amount of light is *setting the aperture*. In video, the same thing is called *setting the iris*. You'd be hard pressed to find a home video camera that *doesn't* have an automatic iris. The important thing is to make sure that the camera also has a manual override.

After switching from automatic to manual, setting the iris is usually done with a knob or slide on the camera. Rarely, it is more like a still camera and is adjusted on the lens.

As with auto white, the automatic iris can be easily fooled. It's going to set itself according to the average light of the scene, which may not be what you want at all. For example, if you are shooting someone standing outside, the bright sky may cause the iris to close down; the face of your subject will then go dark (Fig. 2–12).

Having a monitor—or at least an electronic viewfinder—is important when manually setting the iris. Too much light will wash out the scene. (It could also damage the camera.) Too little and the scene will be dark and have poor color.

What can cause more problems is when the combination of auto iris and auto white are being used. Imagine you are taping a party in

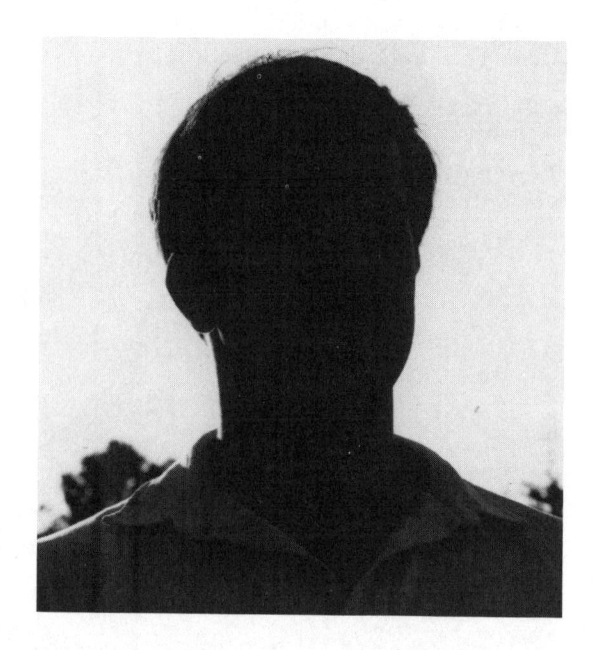

FIG. 2–12 A scene with backlighting only will confuse the auto iris, resulting in a silhouette of your subject.

your living room. The window is open. As you swing the camera through the room, you go across the window. In that instant the camera tries to adjust itself both for the greater light intensity and for the change in color. Between the two, it's common for the scene to momentarily fade, flash, and swing across colors.

AUTOMATIC AND MANUAL FOCUS

Automatic focus is a wonderful advance in photography, since it lets you pay more attention to what you're shooting instead of having to make continuous adjustments. As with other automatic features, it can be fooled. It's going to attempt to focus on the average scene, or on the dominant portion of the scene (Fig. 2–13). For example, if your subject moves off center, the auto focus will focus on whatever was behind him, leaving the subject out of focus.

This automatic feature will also have difficulty with crowds or moving objects. The adjustment isn't instantaneous. In fact, most auto focus features are rather slow.

It's very important that you *never* manually focus the camera while it is set on automatic. You may get away with it once or twice, but eventually you *will* cause damage.

Another feature that is provided with just about every home video camera is a zoom lens, almost always with power zoom for even greater ease in handling. Zoom allows you to get effectively "closer" to your subject without physically moving and comes in very handy for getting a sharp focus. The power zoom feature lets you do this without touching the lens.

Avoid zooming too quickly. The power zoom feature of a camera

FIG. 2–13 The auto focus is on the mountains in the distance, blurring the object you *really* want to have in focus.

FIG. 2–14 To manually focus your camera, be sure the auto focus is shut off; otherwise, you may damage the camera.

FIG. 2–15 Use the macro feature for closeups and small objects.

is "dampered" to prevent this. Full zoom in or out will take a number of seconds. Zooming too fast is irritating to watch. More details on this in Chapter 5.

Some lenses come with a macro feature, allowing a camera to focus on something within a few inches of the lens. On the normal setting, you may not be able to focus clearly on an object closer than 3 or 4 feet. Having a macro feature built into the lens is convenient. You can also buy an accessory lens for the same function (see Chapter 3 for accessory lenses you may find valuable).

CAMERA VS. CAMCORDER

The ultimate in convenience is a camcorder, a camera and recorder all in a single unit. It's heavier than a video camera alone, but lightweight compared to the combination of a camera and VCR. It also requires less power and fewer cables. And it is actually less expensive than buying a separate camera and VCR.

If you already have a portable VCR, a camera may be all you need.

FIG. 2–16 A camcorder is an all-in-one unit, making it the ultimate in carry-along convenience.

FIG. 2–17 A video camera alone is smaller and lighter, but means that your range is limited by cable length.

In this case it is less expensive to get just the camera. Even if your VCR isn't portable, it can be used with a long cable between the camera and VCR—if you don't mind confining yourself to that range.

There are those who claim that separate camera and VCR produce better quality. This may or may not be true, depending on a number of conditions. If the portable VCR by itself carries a price tag of $1500, it probably has higher quality or more features than a camcorder of the same price. A home deck is not meant to be moved around. If you have a fondness for the camera/VTR combination, don't expect your home unit to fulfill the recording half of the job. A portable VCR is designed to operate on standard 12 vdc and is generally built to be a little tougher. (This doesn't mean that it is indestructible.) The pathway and alignment of the tape to the recording heads are critical. Every movement you make can introduce errors in the recording. Whenever possible, set the portable VCR on a firm support of its own. Get an extension cable to attach the camera to it. If you must carry the VCR, keep it tight against your body with short straps, and avoid any sudden movements.

FORMATS

At the moment, you may choose from among four formats: Beta, VHS, VHS-C, and 8mm. Also in the works is a 4mm format. Each has advantages and disadvantages, often determined by personal needs and preferences.

VHS and Beta

The two full-size formats – Beta and VHS – make it easy to blend the camera in with the rest of your system. For example, if you have a VHS video deck, being able to take the tape out of the camera and insert it directly into the home deck can be an advantage. Beta, developed by Sony, first made it possible to build a home VCR. Then JVC

FIG. 2–18 Full-size VHS camcorder (RCA ProWonder CMR300) versus the compact VHS-C camcorder (RCA Small Wonder CPR100). Photo courtesy of RCA.

FIG. 2–19 Two 8mm cameras: Nikon's VN-800, and Minolta's 8 CR-8000S AF. Photo courtesy of Minolta Corp. and Nikon Corp.

developed the VHS format. Since VHS puts less strain on the tapes, it soon began to dominate. When video rental stores sprang up, it made sense for them to concentrate on the VHS format. There were more customers, and the stock of tapes tended to last longer.

Sony answered by greatly improving the Beta format, and including such things as high quality stereo sound. With this, a number of people shifted back to Beta, and there is still a core of users who claim, justifiably, that the quality of both the video and audio are better with Beta.

VHS-HQ increased the quality of VHS reproduction. Zenith sells a camcorder with hi-fi stereo (model VM 7100). Even more recently, SVHS (Super VHS) has become available. According to RCA, the VHS machines have captured about 85% of the total market (including the smaller VHS-C). At the same time, diehards, professionals, and studios tend to stick with the Beta format.

Both "sides" continue to make advances, and the quality you can expect in video equipment will continually increase.

VHS-C and 8mm

VHS-C is smaller than standard VHS. Each cartridge holds 20 minutes of tape at top speed. (European VHS-C is good for 30 minutes, due to differences in camera speed. The blank tapes are compatible, but the recording on them is not.) Some cameras allow multiple speeds, just as home decks do. This increases the overall play time to up to 60 minutes.

Even smaller is 8mm. The tape is just 8 millimeters (about ⅓″) in width. (Other tapes are ½″, with professional studio decks using ¾″ tape.) Because of the smaller size and slower speed, more time can be squeezed onto a single cassette; 8mm tape is not equivalent to standard video tape. It is manufactured in a completely different way (see Chapter 4). The result is that the quality of recording on an 8mm cassette is quite acceptable.

Samsung has announced that it has nearly perfected a video system that uses a tape about half the size of 8mm tape. It's not a true 4mm system, but comes close.

BEFORE YOU BUY

Compatibility

One major concern is that of compatibility with existing equipment. If you have a Sanyo VCR at home, should you buy a Sanyo camcorder? Actually, it doesn't matter. If you use your camera only for shooting, then dub over to the main deck, it doesn't matter if the two are the same format or not. You can dub from a Beta camcorder to a VHS deck just as easily as you can dub from a VHS camcorder to a VHS deck.

However, if you intend to use what you shoot as your original, without dubbing, then it is best to have a camcorder and deck that are both the same format. (You can, of course, run the signal from the camcorder through your deck and then into the television without actually re-recording. And most camcorders allow you to feed directly into the television set.)

One special note worth mentioning; VHS-C cartridges *are* in VHS format. An adaptor is needed, but with this adaptor you can play VHS-C cartridges through a standard VHS machine.

Peripherals are often universally compatible. For example, RCA-type plugs are virtually always used for the audio and video inputs and outputs of home video equipment. The same applies to LLcamcorders, although it is common for the camcorder to have a pinned outlet that connects to the VCR through a provided adaptor cable.

Equipment, such as parts, specific to the make and model of the camcorder won't be the same, regardless of format. For example, you won't be able to plug the viewfinder from a Panasonic onto a Zenith.

Features and Cost

It's important to do a little homework before you buy. By now you have a fair idea of what is available in features and capabilities. Often, the next step is to decide on a price range. It's easy to spend $400 or more for "bells and whistles" – features that are nice to have but that don't have anything to do with the quality of the image. Know before you go to the dealer what you can afford to spend, and what features you can do without to get the needed quality. For example, having a power zoom lens is convenient, but you can save money if you're willing to turn the zoom by hand. Having an in-camera character generator is a wonderful way to embed titles, but if you don't need that sort of thing, why pay for it?

Your first consideration is *image quality*, followed closely by *audio quality*. If that fancy camera with all the features doesn't produce good image and sound, it's no bargain.

How you intend to use the camera determines which features you should look for. Assuming that you are buying through a local dealer, test the camera you have in mind. And test it under a variety of conditions. Try the camera under the showroom lights. Aim it into relatively dark areas, as well as into brighter spots. Then take it outside to see how well it handles full sunlight and full shade. Do an actual recording. Don't just look at the image on a monitor. If the dealer won't allow you to do all this, find another dealer. You *may* have to put down a deposit to prove that you are indeed going to be a buyer once you find the right equipment.

Keep in mind during testing that the results won't be what you'd see on TV. Expect slight imperfections in the image and sound. If you're shooting in a department store, results are likely to be worse than what you'll get at home. To find out just what to expect, and what to accept, try several different cameras of different qualities.

Recording length may or may not be important to you. This can go from the 20 minutes of a single-speed VHS-C camcorder to the 8 hours on slow speed of a camera and multispeed VTR or multispeed camcorder. With rare exception, it is more sensible to think of the recording length range as being from 20 minutes to 2 hours. You can always carry along extra cassettes. Swapping takes just a few seconds. And since they can be used over and over again (most professionals suggest limiting reuse to 50 times), the expense isn't all that bad. A $10, 20-minute tape used 50 times gives you 1000 minutes, or 1¢ per minute. With a $10, 2-hour tape, the cost drops to ⅙th of a cent per minute. Buying six tapes at $10 each may seem like a hefty $60 investment, but it represents a possible 36,000 minutes of taping, even at slow speed.

Mail-Order Purchases

Although the information in this section applies to all purchases, you are perhaps more likely to make a large purchase (and thus get large savings) by using mail order. The primary advantage of buying this way is the savings. Mail-order companies have no actual salesmen, but those who take your order often know more and can even be more helpful than an in-person salesman. A mail-order house doesn't have the overhead expenses of a showroom, and no demo equipment that must later sell for less. Add to this the fact that they deal in considerably larger quantities and you have the potential for discounts up to 50% over what a local dealer has to charge. It's not at all uncommon to save $300 or more on a video camera.

But don't be fooled by the advertised price. This is for the unit only in virtually all cases. It doesn't include shipping or insurance (about 10% of the item price as a general rule of thumb—and it can easily be $100). Some companies tack on a surcharge for use of credit cards (a 6% surcharge on a $1500 purchase is $90).

Many mail-order companies carry two lines. One has been inspected by the company that puts its name on the equipment. The other has been purchased directly from the manufacturer (often overseas) by a private importer. The second is theoretically identical to the first, but will usually cost considerably less. In a real sense, it has an extremely limited, or nonexistent, warranty.

For example, you have your heart set on the RCA CM300 LLcamcorder. This is manufactured in Japan by Hitachi. (In fact, the Hitachi VM5000A is nearly identical.) If the camera has been imported by RCA, it is inspected and tested by RCA before it is made available for sale. This way, the company backs up the unit with its own warranty.

On the other hand, if the camera has been brought into America by a private importer, RCA never sees it. Consequently they won't back the warranty on it. You save, since you don't have to pay the costs of RCA's services for inspection—but you take a chance that the camera will function through the warranty period. It probably will—but if it doesn't, you have no recourse but to pay for repairs yourself. Be sure you understand what you're doing and the risks you are taking. Otherwise, pay the extra for company-imported equipment. In essence, you are then "buying the warranty."

Many mail-order ads carry such wording as "Full U.S.A. Warranty." If that isn't there—and even if it is—ask before you order.

Many of the magazines that carry those ads also make it a point to stay on top of any problems experienced by their readers. If a particular company has been treating readers poorly, or has failed to fill orders, the magazine is likely to refuse to accept its ads. Since mail-order companies do their business through advertising, this is an effective monitor.

Most of the companies are honest and efficient; if one has been around for a long time, you can bet that it gives adequate service and care to its customers. Mail order is also governed by the Federal Trade Commission. State laws, various Federal laws, and U.S. postal laws also apply. All this serves to minimize the risk to you.

Always find out about the return policy of the company. This is particularly important if you're buying equipment without a U.S. warranty. If the equipment arrives and doesn't work, will the company honor its return? How do they handle other problems, such as shipping the wrong equipment?

It's important to keep track of all transactions. Write down the day and time, the order taker's name, and all other pertinent information. If you have to return anything, get a shipping receipt.

For any problems, first contact the company, and preferably the person who took and filled the order. Chances are very good that the problem will be taken care of without hassle. You might even be able to solve the problem on the phone, although a letter with *all* the information is better. Keep a copy.

✔ In Case of Trouble

1. Talk to and/or write to the mail-order company.
2. If you suspect illegal activity, contact the Post Office.
3. Contact appropriate Better Business Bureau, and/or the magazine that carried the ad.
4. Contact The Direct Mail Marketing Association, LLMail Order Action Line (6 E. 43rd St., New York, NY 10017).

If you still can't solve the problem, and you've given the company a fair chance, you have several options. A variety of laws and agencies regulate mail-order business. The Post Office, for example, governs anything and everything that goes through the mail. There are consumer protection agencies both in your area and in the area of the company. You can also contact The Direct Mail Marketing Association (see sidebar).

The law requires that the company stand behind its advertisements. If the ad says that it ships within 24 hours, you should have the equipment in about a week. If the ad says nothing, the law still requires that the company ship within 30 days, or offer you an immediate refund by sending you an option notice. This gives you the choice of canceling the order for a refund, or of accepting a new delivery date. (It is always the shipper's responsibility to trace lost items.)

A refund must be mailed within 7 working days if the order was paid for by cash or check. A credit card refund goes directly to your credit card account. This must be done within one billing cycle (normally 30 days).

Most companies require that you notify them first before returning any equipment. Normally, there is a time limit (10 days is common).

Chapter 3

Peripheral Equipment

Once you own a video camera and VTR (or camcorder combination), you have what you need to make some basic shots. You can get by with nothing more than this. At the same time, there is a variety of equipment you can buy to greatly expand your capabilities and the quality of your recordings, but you'll want to select carefully.

White balance will enable you to make passable recordings with nothing more than available light. But by adding a couple of auxiliary lights, your recordings can be made to look much much more polished. The on-camera microphone that comes with the unit does an okay job. But most people, sooner or later, will want better quality sound—which means a better quality microphone, or a remote microphone, or both. You might even want to own a remote wireless mike.

Then there are video switchers, editors, and enhancers; character generators, graphics generators and sync generators; signal amplifiers and stereo decoders and . . .

LIGHTS

Photography and videography are nothing more than capturing light. Without light, there's no image. With poor light, there's a poor image.

Today's sensitive video cameras can make suitable recordings even in dim light. Normal room light is often sufficient, assuming that you'll be satisfied with somewhat off-color and grainy video.

Having a set of lights can add quality, flexibility, and creativity (see Chapter 6). Even one light can greatly increase the quality. Two or three lights can turn any living room into a home studio. Even if you intend to shoot outside in sunlight for virtually everything, having at least one light can improve the quality of the recorded images. That

FIG. 3–1 A small, on-camera, DC-powered video light from RCA (50-watt VDC050). Photo courtesy of RCA.

FIG. 3–2 A lighting kit from Ambico (V-0817), complete with battery pack. Photo courtesy of Ambico, Inc.

light can be used to soften a harsh sun or fill in shadows, or to light a subject when the background is overpowering.

With lighting equipment you have a number of choices. Your first consideration is where the lights will be used. If they are for inside, the power source can be the AC from a wall outlet. If you want the lights to be portable, they'll have to be DC powered (which means that a battery pack is needed). There are also lights which can be operated from either AC or DC.

As a general rule, DC lamps throw less light than their AC-powered counterparts. (This is not necessarily true with an AC/DC lamp.) The reason is simple. The more light you want, the more power you need. The power you can get from the wall outlet is limited only by the incoming wiring. A standard wall outlet will provide 117 volts AC, and 15 amps, for as long as you pay the electric company.

The power from a battery is considerably more limited. After a relatively short time, the battery will "run dry." The more powerful the light, the faster this will happen (or the larger the battery needed).

Think of a 100-watt lamp operated by the standard 12 volt DC battery pack. The basic power formula is $P = IE$, or the amount of power (in watts) is equal to the current (I) multiplied by the voltage (E). Juggle this a bit and you come to $I = P/E$. The current is equal to the power divided by the voltage.

For that 100-watt lamp to operate on 12 volts, a current flow of 8⅓ amps is needed. At that rate, it won't take long for even the best

FIG. 3–3 One simple, inexpensive means of mounting a light where you need it.

FIG. 3–4 An AC/DC light costs a little more, but is more versatile. This one also has built in "barn doors." Photo courtesy of Ambico, Inc.

battery to empty itself. (With an incoming 117 vac, that same light is going to draw less than 1 amp.)

There's no magical way around this. It's a basic law of electricity. What it comes down to is that DC-powered lights require a decent power pack, and even then can operate only for a limited time.

A little more costly but an excellent system for versatility is an AC/DC light. With these units you have the choice of using a battery to power the light, or to plug it into a wall outlet.

Another choice you'll have is the *kind* of lamp. This isn't quite so important if the lamp will be powered through a wall outlet, but can be critical if the lamp will be powered by a battery. The kinds are tungsten, quartz, HMI and fluorescent.

Incandescent Tungsten

The incandescent tungsten lamp is the least expensive, and the most common. Most of the lamps in your home probably have a tungsten filament. Many standard photo floods or spots also use tungsten. These lamps tend to be large in size and relatively inefficient. However, they have the advantages in cost and in lifespan. The color temperature begins at about 3200°K but decreases as the lamp ages.

Quartz-Halogen Lamps

Quartz lamps—also called halogen lamps—have a tungsten filament inside a tube made of quartz or silica filled with halogen gas. The primary advantage of quartz over tungsten is efficiency. Quartz lamps put out about twice as much light per watt as a standard tungsten lamp. For example, a 60-watt quartz lamp will give off roughly as much light as a 120-watt tungsten lamp. Because of the lower power draw, they are an excellent choice for DC or AC/DC lamps. A second-

FIG. 3–5 A quartz-halogen lamp.

ary advantage is that they maintain their 3200°K color temperature throughout their life.

One disadvantage is that they have a much shorter lifespan (anywhere from about a tenth to half, although they can be made to last longer by reducing the power by about 10%). The lifespan becomes even shorter if you accidentally touch the tube with your finger. The shorter lifespan is made worse by the greater cost of a quartz lamp. A third disadvantage is that they are hotter than comparable tungsten lamps, which means greater care must be taken to avoid burns—both to yourself and to objects near the lamp.

HMI Lamps

Halogen-metal-iodide (HMI) lamps are even smaller and more efficient, putting out about three times as much light per watt as the quartz lamps (and therefore about six times as much light per watt as a tungsten lamp). These lamps have a mercury arc in argon gas within a quartz tube. They require a starter ballast (somewhat similar to a fluorescent tube). These rather expensive lamps burn with a color temperature of 5600°K and simulate sunlight.

Fluorescent Lights

Fluorescent bulbs are rarely used by professionals. In fact, most pros hate fluorescent lights with a passion. Whenever possible, they'll shut them off and use something that can be controlled. The light from fluorescent bulbs is highly diffused and generally not bright enough for a good image. The color temperature is also difficult to control, since it varies across a wide range, depending on the materials used, who made the tube, and even when it was made. The color temperature of fluorescent tubes is higher than incandescent lamps but lower than sunlight. Avoid them whenever possible.

SOUND

On-Camera Microphones

Home video cameras invariably come equipped with an on-camera microphone, fine for some things, but audio quality is usually rather pitiful. And the greater the distance between the microphone and the subject, the more extraneous noise will be introduced. For both higher fidelity and to get only the sounds you want rather than a mixture of sounds, you may wish to invest in an external microphone.

The first thing to do is to look at where the on-camera mike plugs into the camera. What kind of plug is needed? Almost always that will be a pin jack. This is how most video microphones are equipped. If your camera has a different kind of plug than what is on the microphone, adaptors are available.

Another consideration is *impedance.* (It's easiest to think of impedance as being ac resistance.) For maximum benefit, the output impedance of the microphone should be the same as the input impedance of the camera. The reason for this has to do with the way amplifiers and AC signals work, but what *is* important is that, if the impedances are mismatched, the results are going to be poor.

If you use a low-impedance microphone with a high-impedance

FIG. 3–6 Lights will typically use a pin-jack type plug.

FIG. 3–7 Cable adaptors.

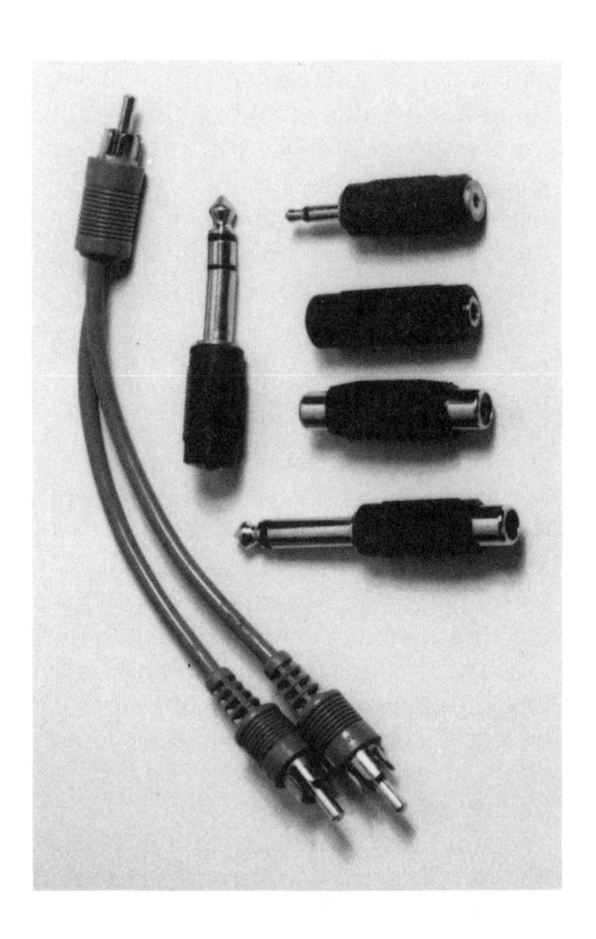

camera, the audio input from that microphone will be fighting an uphill battle. The level of the audio will then go way down, as though the volume had been turned down. On the other hand, a high-impedance microphone feeding a low-impedance input is going to seem as if the volume control had been cranked far beyond the capability of the amplifier. You'll get a badly distorted sound.

The user's manual that came with your camera should list the audio input impedance in the specifications.

There are a number of reasons for using a different microphone than that provided with the camera, not the least of which is improved quality. Almost without fail, the microphone that came with the camera will be omnidirectional, or close to it (see Fig. 5–8). This means that it will pick up sounds that come from anywhere, and especially sounds near the camera. You may wish to simply get a higher quality microphone and keep it on-camera for convenience. This will make your audio sound better, but you will still have limitations. An omnidirectional microphone is an advantage when you want to pick up all sounds. To cut out sounds coming in from the sides, a unidirectional microphone is used.

Zooms, Shotguns, and Remote Mikes

A few companies, such as Ambico, make a *zoom* microphone. These "get closer to the scene" by narrowing the angle of pickup. In effect, the zoom mike is unidirectional.

For even longer audio pickup, a *shotgun* microphone can be used. This specialized mike is built to pick up sounds from a distance while *not* picking up nearby sounds. Even more powerful is a *parabolic audio collector.* This device has a parabolic dish to gather and focus sounds from a great distance away, with the focal point being a sensitive microphone.

The greatest advantage of using a remote microphone is that you can place the mike off the camera and closer to the scene. One very nice accessory to have is a wireless remote microphone. Although somewhat expensive (in the $150 range for a basic unit), the wireless remote allows you to move around without worrying about a cord dangling in the way. A cord is not only a safety hazard at times, it can

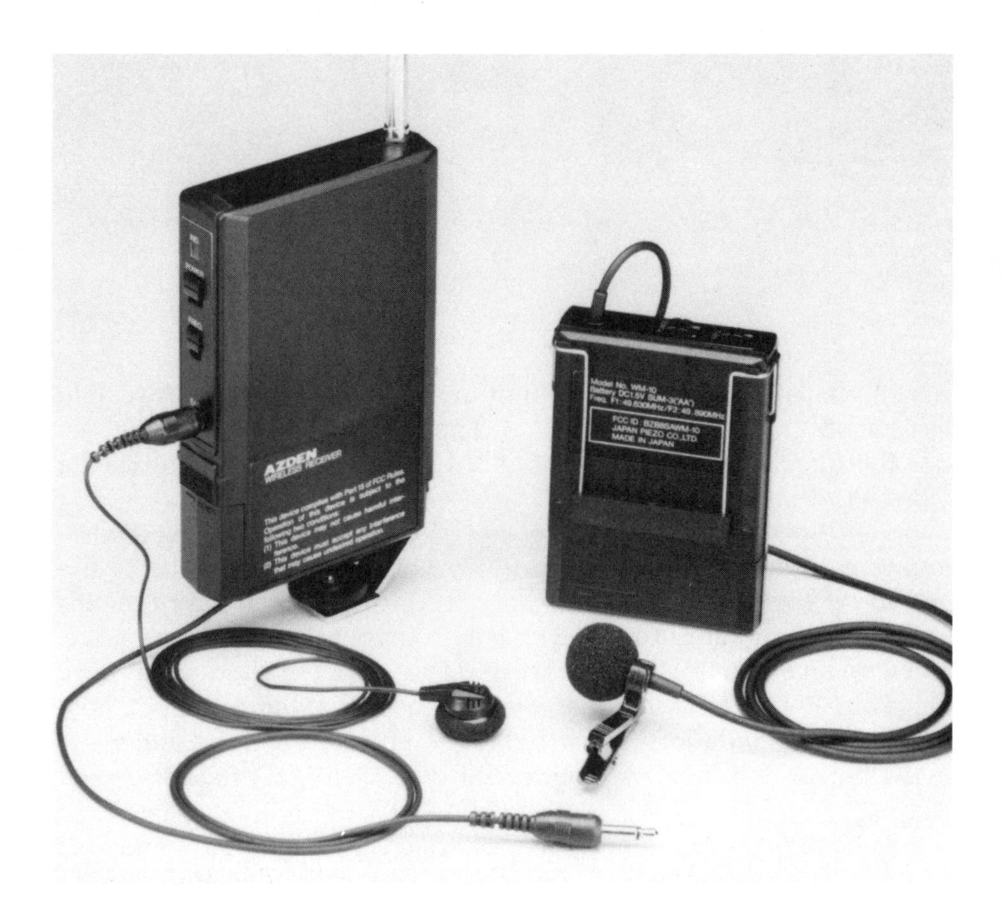

FIG. 3–8 Azden's wireless remote microphone. Photo courtesy of Azden Corp.

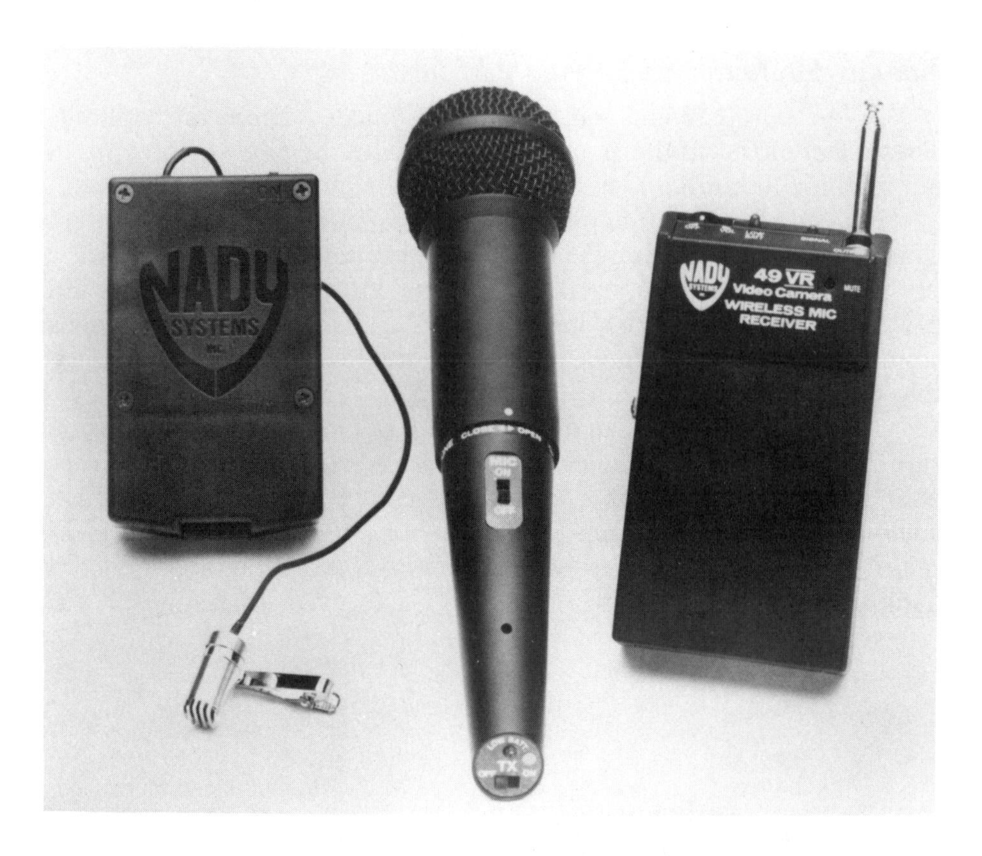

FIG. 3–9 Nady Systems' wireless remote microphone. Photo courtesy of Nady Systems, Inc.

get into the shot—waggling in front of the lens. The wireless remote has a small transmitter built into it. The receiver is built into the section that attaches to the camera. The only thing between is an invisible radio wave.

There are a number of things to consider when choosing a wireless remote microphone. The primary consideration should be the *quality of the sound.* Unfortunately, all too many wireless remotes have an audio quality that is worse than that of the on-camera mike, and with an extremely limited range. Many are advertised as having a range of 100 feet, but what that often means is that the system is capable of sending and receiving at 100 feet—with a lot of noise and static in the signal. The effective range for clear audio might be as little as 20 feet.

The only way to know if a microphone is worth the investment is by testing it. Assuming that you are buying locally, demand a test of the microphone before you buy it. Conditions in the showroom won't be the best for a thorough testing, but you can compare it to the audio you have been getting with another microphone under those same conditions.

ENHANCERS AND PROCESSORS

No matter how good an enhancer or other signal-handling device is, it can't work with a signal that's not there in the first place. If your original image was out of focus, no amount of enhancement or video processing will sharpen it. If it had an overall yellow-green cast and high grain due to poor lighting, the end result through an enhancer won't be much better. It probably is going to be worse.

Think of a scene that has the greenish cast typical of low-light videography. The blues and reds are missing. You can put them in with some enhancers, but they will fill the scene, just as the greens did in the original. By adding red to make someone's face look more normal, you'll also be adding red to the rest of the scene. Add blue to bring out the flowers on the table and . . .

In short, don't expect miracles. And don't expect an enhancer to fix your mistakes. Think of it for what it is—a device that is meant to *enhance* the existing image and/or sound. Typical examples of video enhancer/processor features are color correction, contrast correction, image stabilizing, and image sharpening. An audio processor can reduce noise and hiss, simulate stereo, mix several incoming audio sig-

FIG. 3–10 An image processor and enhancer can help to improve the image. Some can even generate special effects. Here, the FX-1, an expandable system.

nals into a single VCR audio input, and even split the signal so that you can run it to other devices (VCR, home stereo, etc.).

SEG Units

One step up from a enhancer/processor is a unit that can also introduce special effects. This doesn't mean that you can duplicate *Star Wars*. Most home units are fancier and more powerful enhancers with other capabilities built in. For example, there are a variety of ways that you can move from one scene to another. The most common way for the home videographer is to simply stop the camera at the end of one scene and start it again at the next. With the special effects generator (SEG), you can fade the image in and out, often with a number of colors (including black, or no color). You can also "wipe" the screen in various directions and patterns, also with colors.

Many SEG units have a built-in color bar generator. The main function of this is to accurately adjust the television or monitor.

Common with an SEG is the ability to view the image as it normally appears and as it would appear if enhanced. This allows you to preview the effect before you actually record it. (Enhancers sometimes have this feature; SEGs almost always do.)

Higher quality SEGs also have switching built in, so that you can switch between multiple (usually two) inputs and/or multiple outputs. Some even have methods built in to simulate a smooth A/B roll—the combining of two video inputs, such as from two VCRs.

This is more difficult than it sounds. The video tape has a sync track which controls how the VCR and the television (to a lesser extent) work. With two inputs you have two sync tracks. As you switch from one input to the other, the recording VCR drops out of sync for a moment, creating a glitch in the recording. The proper way to handle this problem is to use a "time base corrector," which is a very expensive device that handles the sync of multiple inputs, often by stripping away one or more of the existing syncs and supplying a new one of its own. This is complicated and expensive.

The SEG that offers this usually manages a passable job of it by "going to black" (providing no video signal) or using a cross-channel fade (almost the same thing) for the switching. The glitch is thus minimized.

A character generator or titler may be built in. If not, the unit may have an input so that you can use a computer terminal to create those letters and numbers. (If the particular SEG doesn't have either feature, a separate character generator will be needed.)

Signal Amplifiers

Special signal amplifiers are used primarily to boost a signal so

FIG. 3–11 Ambico's "Super-Duper" VCR output enhancer. Photo courtesy of Ambico, Inc.

that it can be distributed to numerous sources (multiple television sets). These are available at just about any electronics supply store, and even in department or hardware stores.

A more specialized type is used to boost the signal just enough to make up for the signal loss inherent in dubbing, the idea being that the copy will be of a quality near that of the original. Ambico manufactures two models, both called Super-Duper. Model V-0680 handles both stereo and monaural signals. Model V-0660 handles mono only. Both work in much the same way. MFJ has a four-way distribution amplifier that doubles very nicely as a signal amplifier to reduce generation loss (model MFJ-1410). Other distribution amplifiers can be used, and should have separate audio and video connectors in and out (with RCA-type phono being the standard) and preferably should have controls for the amount of amplification (very few will have the latter). Be careful about the amount of amplification; check the level of signal output and compare this with the maximum allowable input to your VCR (usually around 1 volt).

ACCESSORY LENSES AND FILTERS

Your video camera almost certainly came equipped with a zoom lens. This allows you to take a variety of common shots. If the lens also has a macro feature, you will enjoy even more versatility. Even so, there may be times when you'll want something else. Many professional cameras accept interchangeable lenses. The home video camera won't. Instead, there are available screw-on accessory lenses. These work with the existing lens to handle the specific job.

The telephoto zoom on the camera is usually sufficient for getting

FIG. 3–12 *Above,* a variety of lens attachments. *Right,* step-up and step-down rings.

"close" to a subject. If you need to shoot something from an even greater distance, or if your camera is one of the few that doesn't have a zoom, a telephoto attachment can help. Telephoto lenses are rated in power of magnification. A lens rated at 2× means that it will double the apparent size of the image, in effect narrowing the field of view and bringing you twice as close to the subject. With this particular lens, an object 20 feet away will appear to be about 10 feet away; an object 200 feet away will seem to be 100 feet away.

Wide-angle lenses do just the opposite. Their main use is to open the field of view. An example would be trying to shoot a group of people while in the confines of a small room. If you can't move back far enough to get everyone in the frame, a wide-angle lens will "move you back" optically.

A macro attachment is available for close-ups. The lens on your camera may have the ability to focus no closer than 3 or 4 feet. A close-up lens, depending on the power, may allow you to get as close as an inch or so. (Keep in mind that the closer you get, the more difficult focusing will be.)

Also available are a variety of filters. All camera owners should invest in a clear optical attachment to protect the lens. People who own tube cameras should also seriously consider buying a set of neutral density filters. These reduce the amount of light that enters the camera, thus helping to protect the pickup tube when shooting bright scenes.

You can buy filters that color the scene (or parts of the scene). Also available are special effects filters to produce multiple images of the same subject, starbursts, rainbows, vignettes, and so on.

When buying any attachment lens, be sure that the threads of the lens will match those of your camera. In many cases a set of rings will come with the new lens. These are used to adapt the thread size. Those rings that reduce the size (from 55mm to 49mm for example) are *step-down* rings. Those that increase the size (from 55mm to 58mm) are *step-up* rings. The thread size for your camera will be stamped somewhere on the lens, on the sunshade, and usually printed in the manual as well.

SPECIAL-PURPOSE ACCESSORIES

There are so many accessories available that listing and describing them all would be a book in itself. We'll mention a few here.

Tripods

A tripod should be one of the very first things you get. No matter how steady you are, take a tip from the pros and use a tripod whenever possible. Keep the weight of your camera in mind. The tripod has to

FIG. 3–13 A tripod helps to steady the camera; this one is mounted on a dolly, allowing easy movement. Photo courtesy of Bogen Photo Corp.

be large enough and strong enough to support the camera, and anything attached to it, safely. A tripod built to hold a small 35mm camera won't be sturdy enough for a camcorder and its attached battery.

Rewind/Erase Units

Tape rewinders can save wear on your VTR or the motors of your camcorder. At a cost of $40 (and up), it's a lot less expensive to replace several of these than to replace the motors in your VTR just once. It also adds a touch of convenience, especially when it comes to "repacking" tapes (fast forward to the end, then rewind to the beginning).

A few units also have other features, either built in or supplied by attachments. A potentially valuable feature is one that cleans the tape. Unfortunately, most such units clean just one side of the tape, leaving the other side dirty—which can contaminate the tape all over again. (Clean one side, then wind it back and the unclean side will be wound on top of the clean side.) The overall benefits are greatly reduced.

A few even have a means of erasing a tape. This "cleans" the tape in another way by removing any recorded signals, thus returning a tape you've been using for miscellaneous things back to its "virgin" state. The plus is that you get rid of the rainbowing common when putting a new video signal on top of an existing one. If the unit has this feature, it should also have a *built-in safety to prevent accidental erasure.* At very least, the erase mode should be incapable of acting with the record-protect tab removed (it should, of course, be removed from any recording you even *might* want to keep). Preferably it should also have a separate button to activate the erase so that you must purposely and consciously activate the erase.

A unit that only rewinds is of less value. To repack a tape you need to fast forward to the end. Try to find one that can go in both directions. A counter is nice to have, but the chances are close to 100% that it won't match the counter of your VTR, which makes the feature of limited value.

A common problem with too many rewinders is the lack of spring tension on the spindles to pull the tape all the way back inside the cartridge. The easiest solution is for the unit to activate the spool release (through a covered hole in the bottom of the cassette). This would keep the tape inside the cassette at all times. If the unit flips the front flap and pulls the tape out of the cassette for the functions, which is

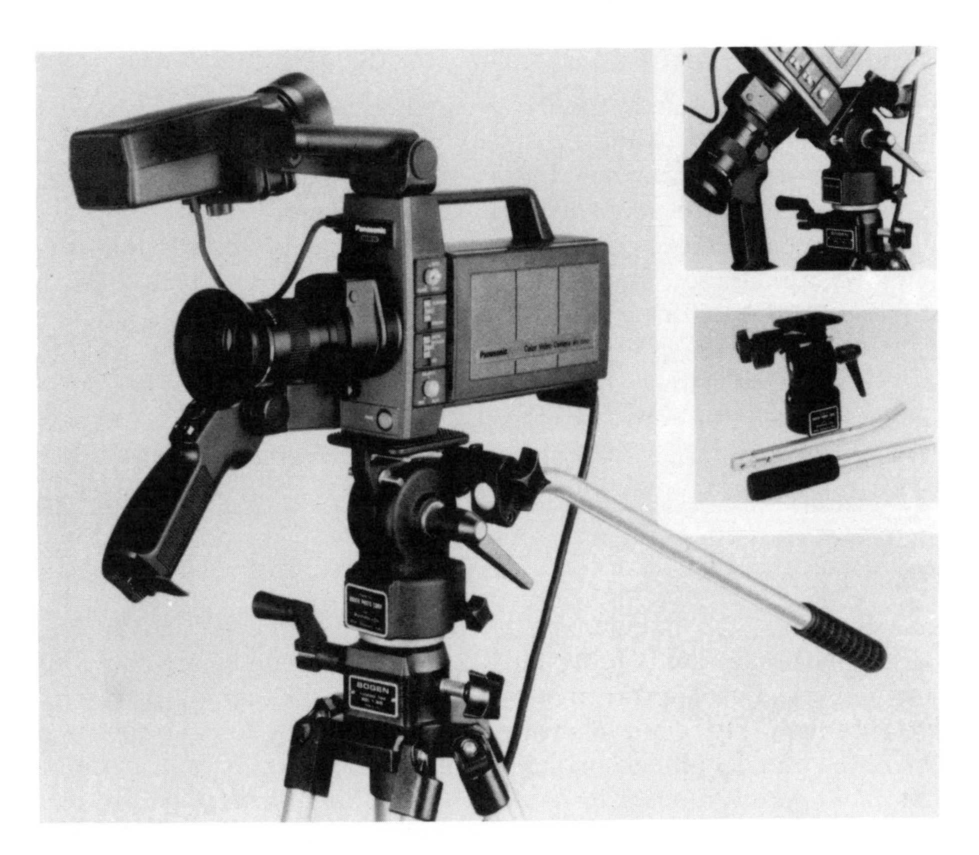

FIG. 3–14 Bogen's tripod head offers such features as fluid pan for smooth movement. Photo courtesy of Bogen Photo Corp.

necessary if the unit is to also clean or erase the tape, spring tension to bring the tape all the way back inside the cartridge is important. Without it, when you remove the tape from the machine, the flap will shut down on top of exposed tape, damaging it.

You want a unit you can control; many have an "on" switch to activate, but no way to stop it other than the built-in automatic switch. Other models don't even have an on/off switch for the power. The only way to remove power in such units is to unplug it from the wall outlet.

Also, be very careful in choosing a multifeatured rewinder. Quite often they are overpriced. You can often buy a rewinder and a bulk tape eraser for less, while ending up with higher quality and better convenience. A few units are strictly battery powered. You might save $10 or so in the initial outlay, but you'll use that up quickly in the cost of batteries. The unit you buy should run on a standard AC wall outlet, even if that means using an AC-to-DC adaptor (which should be included, and not as a separate "accessory" purchase). The battery-powered capability is fine—even an advantage—but it shouldn't be the only choice.

Equipment Protection

Carrying cases and bags are worthwhile investments to keep your equipment organized and protected! A simple canvas bag will help keep your equipment clean, but a hard case does a better job of dust prevention and protection from physical damage.

Some customized cases have cutaway compartments to hold specific equipment. Or, you can adapt a case to your equipment. With some careful measuring and cutting of the foam cushioning, you can customize the case yourself.

It's advisable to use bags or cases for the rest of your video equipment, too. Banging around a video light can ruin it in a hurry. Lugging around a handful of loose cables can be troublesome. A bag or case will organize and protect this equipment, and make it much easier on you.

Converters

If you've been taking home movies for some time, it might be nice to change those over to video tape. You can make do by shining your movie projector on a screen or white card and videographing it with your camera. You could also spend a lot of money to have someone make the transfer (and even blend in an audio track). Or you can transfer those home movies to share with the rest of your family and friends. Converters (to go from movie, slide, or print to video tape) aren't as expensive as you might think!

FIG. 3–15 A movie-to-tape converter with a built-in macro feature. Photo courtesy of Ambico, Inc.

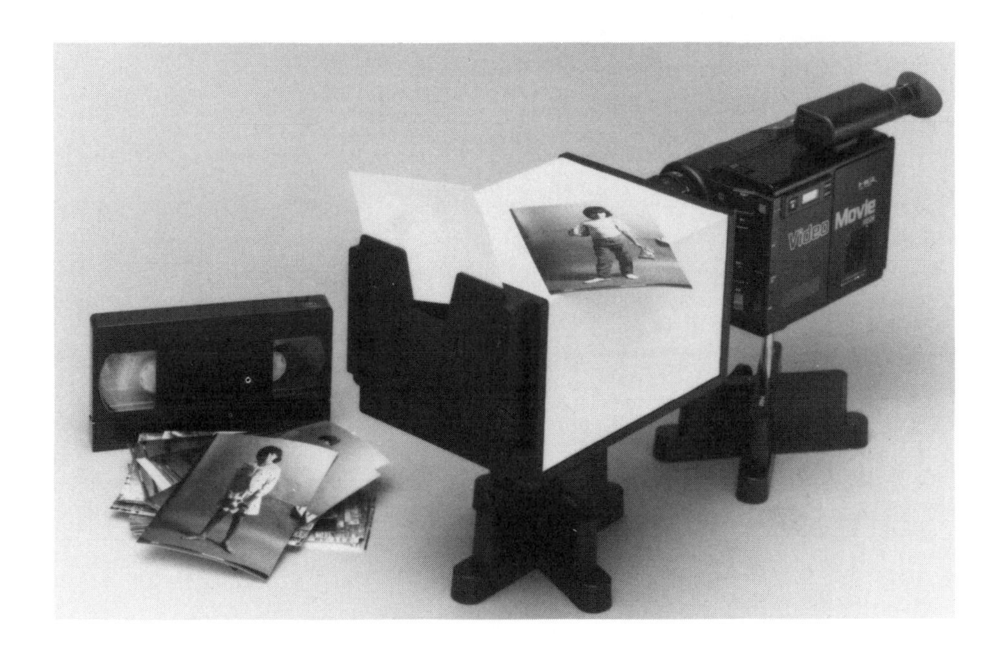

FIG. 3–16 Transferring photographic prints to video tape. Photo courtesy of Ambico, Inc.

Battery Packs

The battery that comes with your camera or camcorder might be fine for "average" shooting. It may hold enough to power the camera or camcorder for anything from 20 minutes to about an hour. If you also need to power a light or want to be sure that you will have plenty of power for a longer shooting session, you can buy an external battery pack. (The first time you have to stop taping for 8 hours to let the battery recharge after just 30 minutes of taping can drive the importance home in an unforgettable way.)

To be of maximum versatility, the battery pack should be relatively small and light, and you should be able to of attach it to your belt. Preferably the pack should have an indicator to tell you how much power is left in the pack. It should also have an automatic shut-off to prevent overcharging.

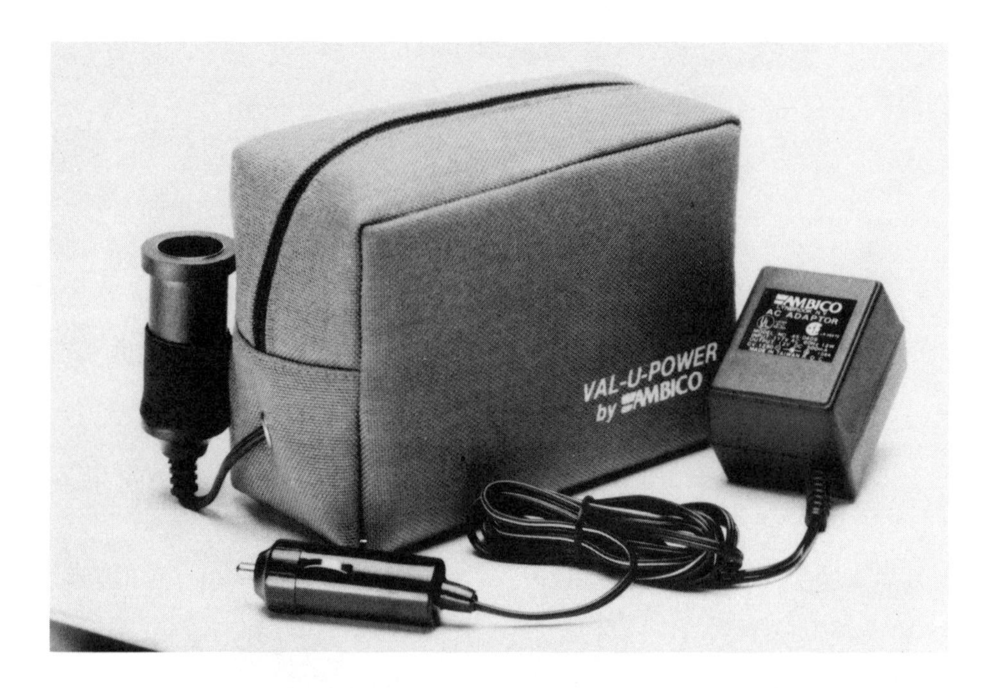

FIG. 3–17 A rechargeable external battery pack such as Ambico's Val-U-Power, can be used to extend operating time or to power portable lights. Photo courtesy of Ambico, Inc.

Chapter 4

Video Tapes and Cartridges

Reel-to-reel tapes were required by the first video machines. These reels were large, heavy, difficult to handle—*and expensive!* There are still professional video decks today that use reel-to-reel tapes, although many have changed over to cassettes. Home decks and camcorders always use the handier and less expensive cartridges.

The introduction of cassette tapes proved a major boon, making it possible to mass-produce equipment that is both relatively inexpensive and simple to operate. As an added advantage, when the tape is held inside a permanent container, it is better protected.

The cassette is pushed into the slot of the camcorder or VCR. An arm unhinges the front flap of the cassette, and then a mechanism pulls the tape out and winds it along the tape guides and across the heads. This is done automatically, and without the need for tedious feeding of the tape by hand. Your fingers never touch the tape.

Many VCR and camera owners have been thoroughly forewarned that the most frequent cause of problems is dirty heads, or dust or moisture inside the machine. Most users are *not* aware of the fact that over half of the problems are actually caused by faulty cassettes. In return, a dirty machine is the single greatest cause of the machine "eating" the tape.

The cassette is a relatively delicate mechanism. In order to be as inexpensive as possible, the plastic construction is not extremely sturdy. It is very easy for the spring-loaded protective flap, or the plastic hubs or ratchets that allow the tape to move back and forth inside the cassette, to become broken or to shift out of alignment. If the cassette is not functioning properly, the machine will not be able to load the tape. A bad cassette can even damage the machine.

SOME IMPORTANT PRECAUTIONS

Improper storage can ruin video tapes and even damage a VCR. A few common sense precautions will greatly increase the life of both tape and machine.

Moisture and Temperature

Moisture or condensation can cause immediate deterioration in the cassette and in a VCR. In order to reduce such accidental moisture, be sure the video cassette is kept at room temperature for at least one hour before being used. If a cassette has been outside on a cold winter evening, don't immediately put it into the warm camera. It can result in the formation of dew (condensation). This moisture on the tape can damage the tape and can also be rubbed from the tape onto the delicate recording/playback heads and other inner mechanisms of the VCR.

Store cassettes *only* in a cool, dry place. They are sensitive to heat as well as cold. More than one owner has lost a valued recording by leaving the cassette in the car on a hot day. Others have damaged their prize recordings by carelessly placing them on radiators or too near heater vent outlets. Some have found themselves having to pay for rented movies accidentally destroyed by such carelessness. Even if the heat doesn't melt the cassette, strong sunlight and heat can degrade or ruin the recording.

Storage

Store cassettes in the cardboard or plastic boxes they came in when you bought them. You can also buy special video cassette storage cases, preferably the type that has doors or drawers that close tightly.

Cassettes should be stored vertically or horizontally (on edge).

✔ Cassette Care

Avoid exposure to heat, moisture, and magnetism
Don't use a cassette until it has reached room temperature
Don't bump or jar the cassettes
Rewind completely before storage
Store in a cool, dry place
Keep the cassettes in their boxes, and away from dust
Store vertically or horizontally only—never flat
Never touch the tape
Fast forward and rewind all new or "suspect" tapes

Never keep a cassette flat for extended storage: this can cause the edges of the tape to bend, thus ruining either the audio or the cue track.

Naturally, take care to prevent shock damage to cassettes. Don't drop them, or bang them around. The cassettes are tough, but they're far from being indestructible.

Keep cassettes away from any magnetic field. One person set a cassette containing a favorite movie on the speaker of his stereo. When he went to play the movie, he couldn't figure out why it was suddenly gone. Electric motors, power transformers, and other such devices generate magnetic fields. Keep the cassettes well away from these and other suspected sources.

Fully rewind a tape before storing it. *Do not* store cassettes for more than short periods without rewinding back to the beginning of the tape.

If a tape has been stored for a long time, and when you buy a new tape, it is best to fast forward the cassette all the way to the end, and then rewind it before playing. This repacks the tape properly, and will also help to avoid sticking or moisture problems.

Never touch the surface of the tape. The hinged flap is there to keep tape from being exposed when it is not in the machine. Fingerprints and oils from your skin can ruin a tape very quickly. Dirt and grease can also damage the delicate internal mechanisms of the VCR itself.

ANATOMY OF A CASSETTE

The cassette or cartridge is a protective plastic box with the tape inside ready for immediate use. The cassette contains two reels, onto which the tape is wound and transferred.

If you look at the back edge of the tape cassette (the side that is inserted into the VCR) you can see that the tape stretched between the two reels is protected by a hinged door, or flap (Fig. 4–1). When the cassette is not in the machine, a spring-load keeps this flap down, keeping the tape protected from fingers and other dangers.

On the righthand side of the cassette, you'll find a small button. This is the release catch for the hinged flap. The VCR automatically presses this button to release the door to allow access to the tape. You can also release the door manually by pressing this button.

The underside of the cassette has a small hole (Fig. 4–2). Whether a VCR is front-loaded or top-loaded, these small holes allow pins from the machine to slip into the cassette. The door is released, and the tape is fed into the VCR.

On the rear edge, opposite the hinged door, is a removable tab that may be broken off by pushing or prying it with your finger or with a

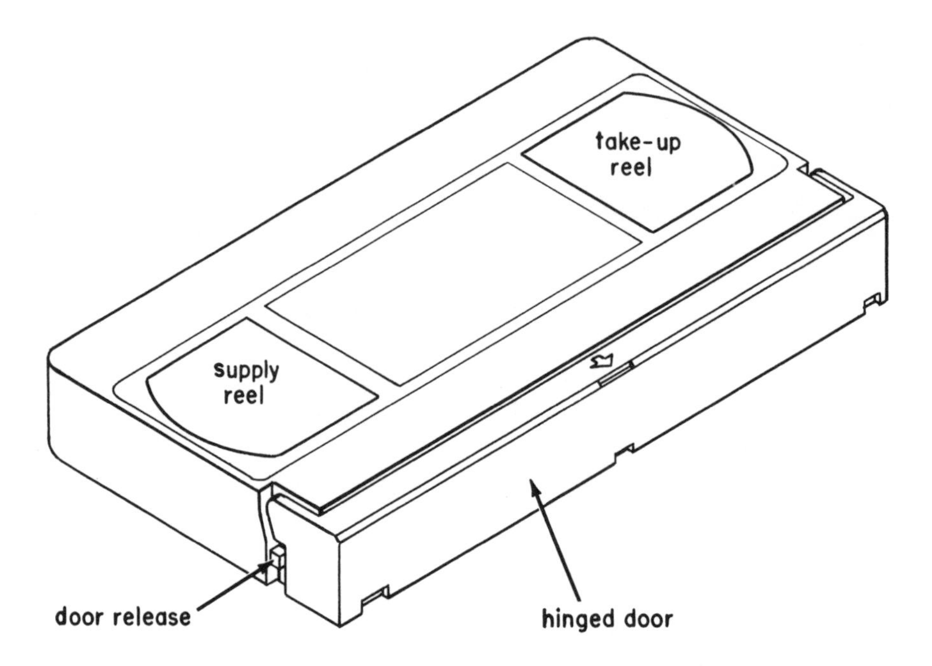

FIG. 4–1 Top view of a cassette.

screwdriver. After the tab has been removed, the cassette can be used for *playback only,* and any material which has been recorded is protected from being erased. If at some time you decide that you *want* to record on that cassette, merely cover the hole (carefully) with a piece of adhesive tape.

Loading Cassettes

When a cassette is inserted into a VCR, whether front-loading or top-loading, the tape is pulled out of the cassette and threaded inside the machine through an arrangement of levers. The entire operation is completely automatic. Because of this automatic feature and the simplicity of the cassettes, the mechanics of the VCR unit are more complicated than those of the reel-to-reel video tape machines. A complex system of levers, rods, and servo-mechanisms make up the mechanics of the VCR. And the number of electronic circuits needed to control the mechanics make the recorder more complicated for servicing than the older, more basic units.

When a cassette is brought into position inside the VCR, the pro-

Warning

Cassettes must be inserted into the recorder with the label up. They cannot be used upside-down.

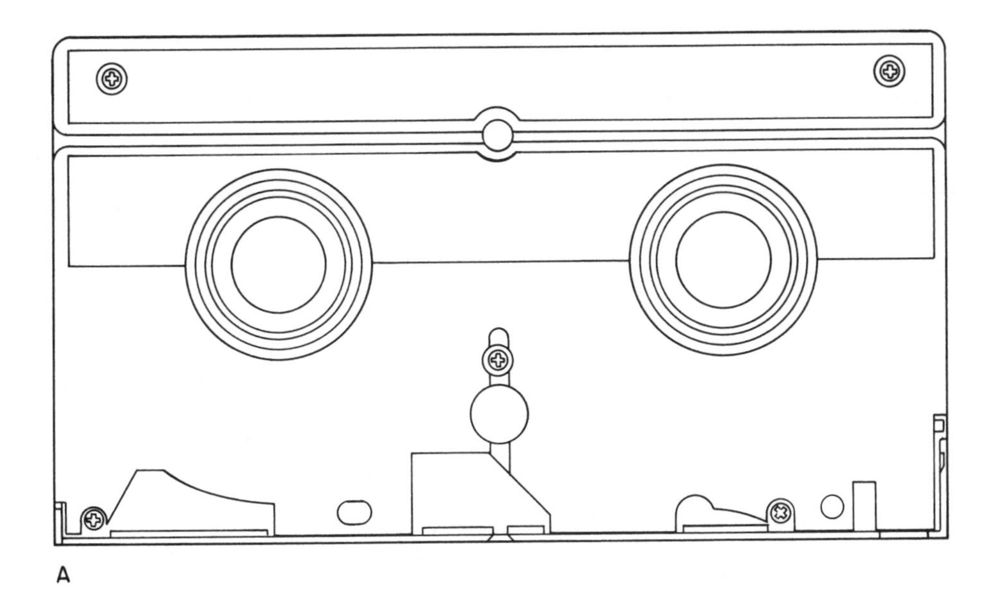

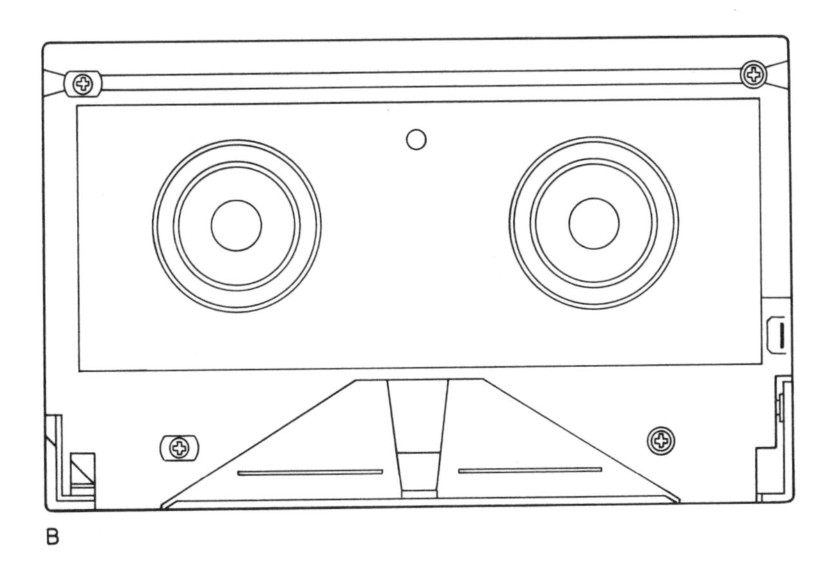

FIG. 4–2 Bottom view of VHS (A) and Beta (B) cassettes.

tective door of the cassette is lifted open and the cassette is lowered over a vertical metal pin. This pin is on an arm or lever which is attached to a large circular ring called a *threading ring.* When the VCR is used for playback or in fast forward, the ring rotates and causes the arm and pin to pull the tape out of the cassette and around the threading path across the heads. When the threading has been completed, the threading motor stops and a solenoid is used to clamp the pinch roller against the capstan. The tape now begins moving in its normal direction along the tape guides and across the rotating head.

When your cassette is first inserted into the machine and is threading, don't touch the other controls. In a sense, this is like trying to force the tape and mechanisms in two directions, or two speeds, at the same time. Most modern VCRs have protective devices that prevent the controls from operating while the tape is threading, but it is still possible to damage the machine or tape by pushing the selector switches while the cassette is threading.

Once the threading is complete, the function buttons operate and there is no danger of damaging the tape or machine. This threading usually takes no more than 2 or 3 seconds.

Whenever a stop button is pushed, the threading ring rotates, unwinding the tape from across the heads and the tape guides, then placing it back inside the cassette. Often, springs beneath the reel spindles will twist the reels in opposite directions to complete the job.

Fast forward or fast rewind are usually accomplished with the tape inside the cassette, without the tape crossing the heads. (This causes excessive wear both to the tape and to the VCR.) Stop frame and other specialized custom functions take place while the tape stays in its ready position around the rotating heads, no matter what the mode of operation.

Remember that, as the cassette goes into the machine, the protective flap on the cassette is lifted to expose the tape. Because of this, video cassettes should not be left in the VCR when they are not in use. When the stop button is hit at the end of a playback or record function, the cassette should be removed before the machine is turned off.

TAPE REPAIR

There is a common and false belief that video cassettes cannot be spliced or repaired. Actually it's not only possible to repair a tape, it's easy.

Cutting or Splicing

The simplest method is to sacrifice some of the tape. This involves unwinding and discarding the tape on one side of the damage. Release the protective flap. Depending on the cartridge, you may have to release the catch that holds the reel. This is usually done by inserting something, such as a pencil, in a hole on the bottom of the cassette.

Now cut the tape and pull it out from the side to be discarded. This is normally the shortest side, but which side you throw away will obviously depend on which is more important to you. Make the second cut at the clear leader. (Don't remove that leader. The VTR needs

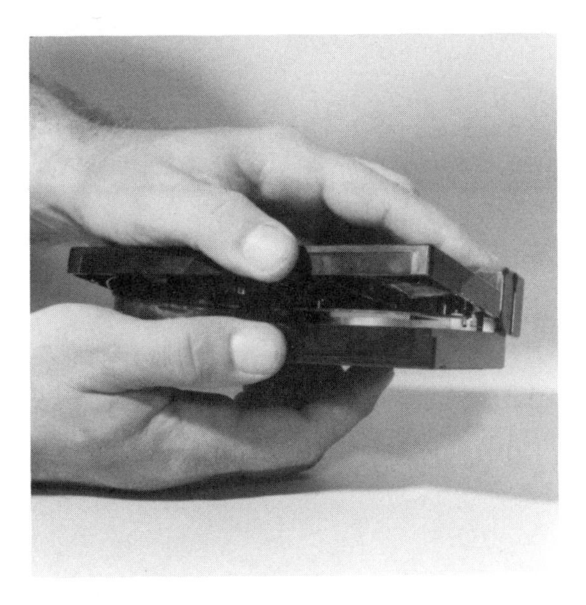

FIG. 4–3 Separate the base from the lid, taking note of the location of springs, tabs, and screws.

FIG. 4–4 Remove the tape from the smallest (most nearly empty) spool.

it.) Finally, use adhesive tape to attach the good end of the video tape to the leader.

If all the tape is of value to you, you have two choices. One is to wind the removed tape onto another cartridge, which usually means that you'll have to waste the good tape in that cartridge. The second method involves splicing. This means that you'll be attaching video tape to video tape, rather than to the leader. Extreme care must be taken. The only time you should attempt to splice the video tape is if the material on the tape is more important to you than the VCR itself, or the possible repair bill to replace the heads.

In a sense, splicing means that you're "breaking the rules."

First, you'll be handling the tape. Doing so is risky. To reduce the risk, get some lint-free gloves, such as those used by photographers.

✔ **Warning**

Although splicing is possible, it should be used as a last resort only! Splicing can cause damage to the VCR heads.

You can buy these at many photographic supply stores for just a few dollars.

Second, you're putting glue on video tape that will be passing over the heads inside the VCR. When you splice into the leader, the tape will pass through the machine, but—if you do the job right—*not* over the heads. If any of the adhesive gets on the heads or onto other delicate parts, you're facing an expensive repair bill.

Third, even with a careful splice there will be at least one spot on

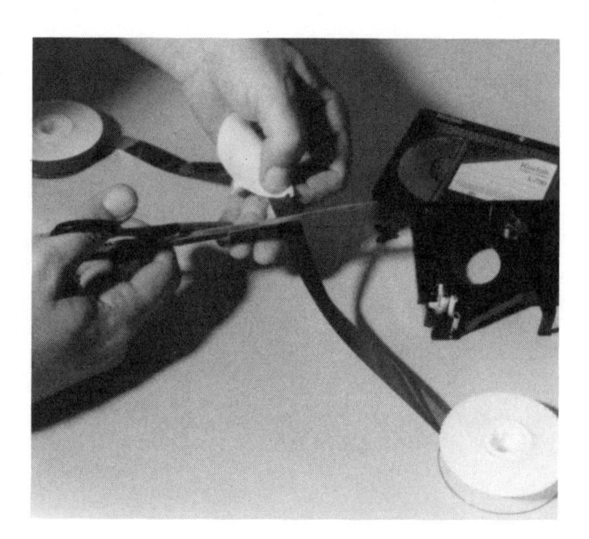

FIG. 4–5 Trim the broken end of the tape to be saved.

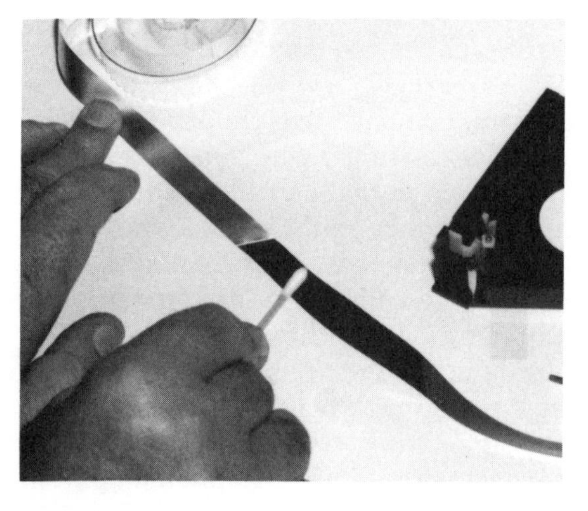

FIG. 4–6 Attach the tape to the leader.

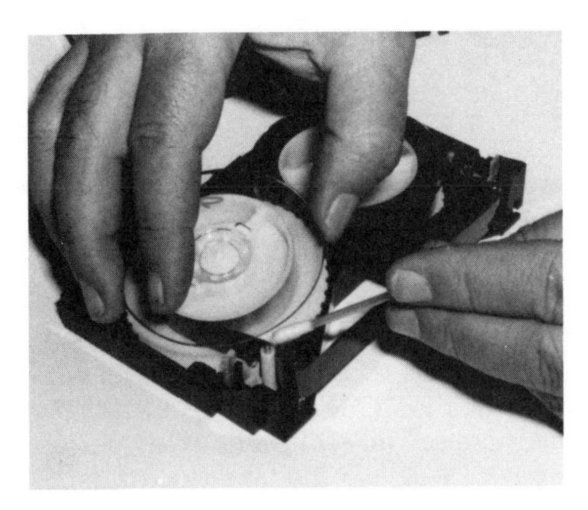

FIG. 4–7 Carefully reassemble the cassette.

the tape that is thicker than the others, and the chance that there will be "sharp" edges. Either can cause physical damage to the machine.

Splicing video tape is to be avoided whenever possible. For the safety of the machine, you're better off to try every other method first, including dubbing the original. (Dub to the damaged area, pause the recording VTR through the damage, and dub to the end.)

If splicing is the only possible solution, proceed carefully. And once you've completed the job, make a copy of that tape (assuming that it is legal to do so) and place the spliced copy in storage as an "emergency backup." The fewer times you run it through the machine, the less chance there will be of the splice causing damage. Preferably, the only time that tape should go through the VCR is when you're making the dub.

Make the first cut where it is needed, and a second cut if necessary. The two ends should be *perfectly clean and flat.* Then overlap the two ends and make a straight diagonal cut. This is to allow the ends to mesh perfectly. Line the two ends up so that the ends are perfectly flat against each other, and so that the tape is in a perfectly straight line. Finally, use splicing tape to attach the two ends together.

Swapping Cassettes

If you have a damaged cartridge, but the tape is fine, the easy solution is a tape swap. Find (or buy) a new cartridge, discard the tape inside and replace it with the recorded tape from the damaged cartridge.

The best method for swapping is to take the cassettes apart. Most are held together with six or seven small Phillips head screws through the bottom of the case. If these screws are carefully removed, the tape case may be taken apart. Take note of any springs or plastic tabs held in place by the pressure of the lid against the base. It is best to make sketches so you'll know exactly how everything goes back together. And keep in mind that your fingers should *never* touch the tape.

This swap will also tell you if a malfunction was caused by the cassette case itself or by the tape. In many instances, the springs, tabs, or support posts inside the cassette will have slipped out of position, or become bent or broken.

Untangling Tape

The single most common cause of tape damage is dirt, both on the tape and in the VCR. If those loading/unloading mechanisms get dirty, they're not going to be able to do their job. One result can be that a part of the tape is left outside the cassette and still partially in the tape path. When the cassette is ejected, it leaves the tape behind. If that weren't bad enough, the flap on the cassette closes as the cassette ejects, clamping down on the tape and causing even more damage.

The easy solution is to learn the sounds your machine makes. My own VCR makes a distinctive click when the tape has been successfully unthreaded and put back into the cassette. If it doesn't make that particular sound, I know that a piece of the tape is still outside the cassette (and that it's time for a thorough cleaning). Ejecting the tape at that point is only going to make matters worse.

Listen to your own VCR, including the VCR section of your camcorder. Become accustomed to the sounds it makes, and when it makes them. Pay conscious attention to this for awhile until it becomes automatic. An unusual sound, or the lack of a normal sound, will let you know that something is wrong.

If the tape hasn't gone back into the cassette, all you have to do is to repeat the Play–Stop sequence. If the tape didn't get all the way back into the cassette the first time, it might the second. If it doesn't after a few tries, shut off the power. In many machines, taking away the power reduces or removes tension on the tape and allows the springs in the spindles to pull the tape inside the cassette.

Depending on your machine, you may or may not be able to complete the unthreading by activating either fast forward or rewind. However, there is a risk involved. If the tape is badly tangled due to some other cause, going into one of the fast motion functions can cause damage to the tape and to the VCR.

A very good idea is to open the VCR (if possible) and visually examine the situation. For a front-loading machine, this means removing the upper cabinet and most likely a cover plate inside.

For a top loader, you may be able to see enough just by looking. You can often get at the tangle by merely removing the small top cover, which is normally quite easy. With a front-loading machine, and with some top loaders, you may have to completely remove the top part of the cabinet to get at the tangle. If you find that you have to touch the tape, do so only while wearing lint-free gloves. Once the cassette is completely removed from the machine, check it carefully for any crinkling or other damage. The bad tape should be pulled out from both reels through the hinged flap and cut off. (See "Cutting or Splicing" earlier in this chapter.)

BUYING TAPES

Everyone knows someone who has the "save money" bug so bad that he'll spend $10 in gas to save 10¢, or who is constantly spending to make up for "saving" on second-rate products. Some savings are not so valuable after all, and that pertains particularly to the quality of recording tape used in your VCR unit.

When plastic tape is manufactured, there are several grades in the milling process. The best grades are generally used for video and delicate computer recording media. Sometimes economy grades will work in a VCR recorder, but will not last as long as the better quality tapes, and are more likely to cause excessive wear to the heads and transport mechanisms. Unfortunately, some "bargain brand" tapes are so poorly made that they leave behind flakes of the oxide coating or cause other damage.

Use of quality recording tape will lengthen the life of your machine. The better tape will also last longer and cause fewer problems. Stay away from the so-called "bargain brands." In general, so long as you stick with well-known brand names, you're likely to end up with decent and reliable tapes and cassettes.

Chapter 5

Operating Your Equipment Professionally

Put an amateur behind the best video equipment and you'll still get an amateur production. But put an amateur-quality camera in the hands of an experienced professional and the end recording is going to be good.

Equipment quality *is* important: obviously, a top-notch camera is going to do a better job than a cheapie. But even the very best equipment isn't going to produce much if you don't operate it correctly. Many of today's video cameras have automatic features to take care of a large part of the job. Auto white, for example, will adjust the camera for the color temperature of the lights. An auto iris will open or close the lens, depending on the amount of light. Auto focus will keep the subject sharp without effort on your part.

But the greatest mistake amateurs make is to rely too heavily on those automatic features. Each can be "fooled." Auto focus is wonderful for keeping your hands free, but if it's centering on something in the distance, your main subject is going to be blurred. And if the background is bright, an auto iris might set the camera for that, causing what you *want* to record to be thrown into darkness.

Learn the features of your equipment, how to operate those features, and also what the limitations are.

USING LIGHT AND COLOR TO ADVANTAGE

Your eyes adapt automatically to a variety of lighting conditions. A yellow shirt and natural skin tones will look fine to you in the sun, in the shade, or inside. Even in relatively dim light, your eyes will be able to pick up considerable detail.

The same is *not* true of a camera. Set the camera for sunlight and anything in the shadows will begin to turn blue. In the living room everything will shift toward red. In dim light, reds and blues will start to disappear, causing a greenish appearance with a loss of detail and an increase in "grain."

You eye won't see any of that. Not until you play back the recording.

A tungsten filament gives off light with a color temperature of about 3200K. This is considerably more red than sunlight at noon (approximately 5600K) but is fairly close to the color of light later in the day (due to the angle of the sun). On a cloudy day, or in the shadows, the color temperature is closer to 6500K, which makes it much more blue.

COMPARING LIGHT SOURCES

Light Source	*Color Temperature*	*Effect Compared to Sun*
Tungsten	3200°K	red
Fluorescent	4500°K	greenish
Sun	5600°K	–
Shade	6500°K	blue

Quite often, you'll find yourself shooting under conditions of mixed light sources. You might be outside with part of the scene in full sunlight and part in the shadow of a tree. Or you might be inside, with some light coming from lamps in the room and some sunlight coming in through the window. An understanding of what this means is important (see Comparing Light Sources).

Take the first example—sunlight and shade. If the camera is set for the sun, anything in the shadows will have a bluish cast. Set the camera so that colors in the shade are correct, and everything out in the sun becomes more red. If you set the camera halfway between, the sunlit parts will still be red and the parts in the shade will still be blue (less so, but with neither being color correct). The solution is to avoid scenes with mixed lighting.

Learn how to set the color balance control—the white balance—on your camera. Remember, the three primaries are red, green, and blue (RGB). All colors recording and played back are composed of these three primaries. An equal combination of all three makes white. Theoretically, if you can balance the camera to read a true white, the

FIG. 5–1 A small, portable color television, preferably one that can be powered with batteries, will be of great help in testing and adjusting white balance.

three primaries will also be correct, which in turn means that all colors will be correct.

Setting the white balance properly depends on the color of light being used. Your camera may have designations for different kinds of lighting, but very few are accurate. The marked settings are *approximations only*. For example, when set to the incandescent lamp marking, the end recording may be too red or too blue. This problem is made worse by slightly different colors put out even by lamps of the same type. The incandescent bulb in the table lamp will have a slightly different color temperature than the professional incandescent photoflood. Both will decrease in color temperature as they age.

Take the time to learn the characteristics of your own camera. The correct setting for a certain scene may be two marked dots to the right with your camera, while your friend's camera will need one dot to the left for accuracy.

Even if you think you know exactly where to set the balance, the only reliable way to adjust white balance is by using a portable color monitor. Small, battery-powered portable color televisions are fairly expensive ($200 and up). If you plan to do a lot of taping under a variety of conditions, it can be a wise investment. Obviously, the little TV must be of sufficient quality to display colors accurately.

LEARNING HOW TO FOCUS

Sharp focusing with a video camera is considerably more difficult for most people than with a still camera. A large part of the problem is the viewfinder. In a still camera, the viewfinder is optical and often has some kind of focusing guide built in. It may have a split-image finder, with sharp focus assured when the separated lines come together. Or it may use a grid that is obvious until the camera has been properly focused, at which time the grid disappears.

With a home video camera, the viewfinder is a miniature b&w television. There are rarely any guides to help you focus. Normally, all you can do is judge whether or not the image you're seeing in the tiny monitor is at maximum clarity. With many video viewfinders, this can be extremely difficult to do accurately. You can make it easier on yourself with a few tricks.

Depth-of-Field

The easiest is the choice of lens or lens setting. A wider angle lens will have better depth-of-field than a telephoto lens. (Depth-of-field is the range at which an object will be in focus.) For example, at the widest setting on your zoom lens, an object anywhere between 10 and 24 feet might be in near-perfect focus. That gives you a range of 14 feet.

As you zoom in, the lens becomes more and more a telephoto lens, and depth-of-field decreases accordingly. At full zoom and the same focus setting, that same camera might have a depth of field of only 12 to 15 feet. What *was* in focus at 20 feet from the camera will go out of focus due to the change in depth-of-field as you zoomed in.

Another factor is the iris opening. The wider the opening, the shallower the depth-of-field (Fig. 5–3). As the amount of light decreases, the iris must open wider to allow a decent image. Conversely, the brighter the light, the smaller the iris and the greater the depth-of-field.

Place an object 8 feet from the camera and set the lens for whatever angle you wish to use (zoom in or zoom out). With full and bright sunlight, anything from 4 to 15 feet can be in focus (depending on the camera and lens). Wait until late evening when the sunlight has nearly disappeared and the iris will have to open wider. Now perhaps only those things in the range of 7 to 9 feet will be in focus.

You'll notice this effect yourself when you shoot scenes outside. Under bright sun, the depth-of-field increases so that more things are in sharp focus. The entire scene looks sharper simply because the depth-of-field is deeper. Back inside with dimmer lights, focus will be more difficult to maintain, with more things out of focus. With all else being equal, something placed 5 feet behind the main subject outside could be in perfect focus, while the same object at the same distance indoors will be a blurry haze.

In short, a wider angle and brighter lighting contribute to easier focusing by increasing the depth-of-field for the lens. The two work together. In bright sunlight, the almost-closed iris can provide enough depth-of-field so that even at full zoom you'll find focusing easy. At

FIG. 5–2 Depth-of-field—or the range of sharp focus—depends on the angle of the lens. A wider angle lens provides greater depth-of-field.

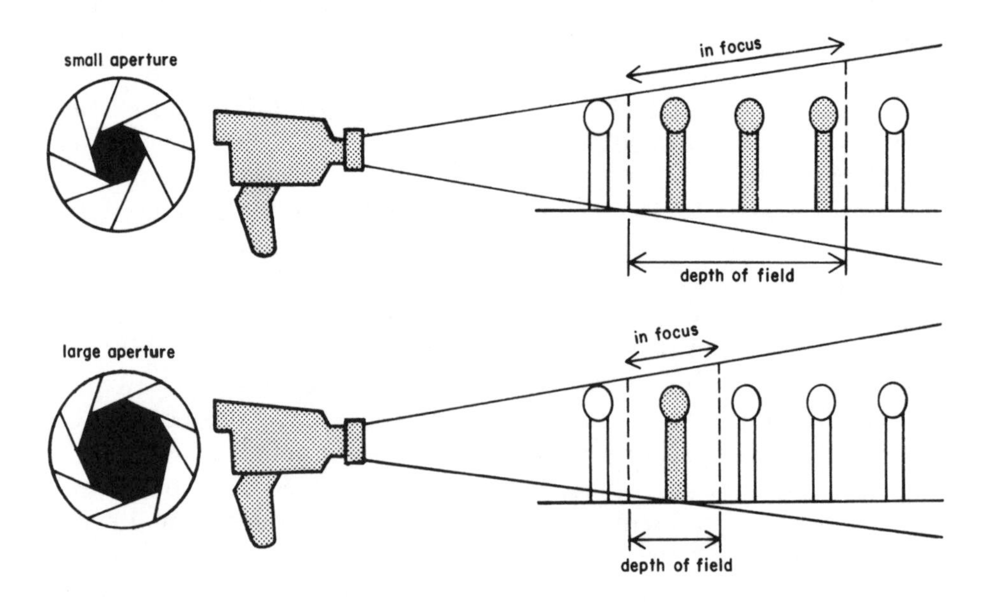

FIG. 5–3 A larger iris opening *decreases* depth-of-field.

the same time, using full zoom in dim light is going to provide such a shallow depth-of-field that the range of sharp focus might be only a few inches and almost everything will be blurry.

The professional will always provide adequate light and move closer to the subject, rather than zoom in. Obviously, there are times when you have little choice. You may not be able to move closer. That's what a zoom lens (or a telephoto lens) is for. Likewise, there will be times when you either shoot under imperfect lighting conditions or not at all. The goal is to at least not have both factors working against you at the same time.

The zoom of your camera is a handy feature and, with experience, can be used as a focusing aid. Trying to focus on something 20 feet away can be difficult. By zooming in, you make the subject effectively larger (usually with a 6:1 ratio), which in turn makes it easier to adjust the focus (Fig. 5–4). Once you have the subject in focus, you can go back to the wider angle.

Auto Focus

Automatic features can be easily fooled by circumstances. This is apparent with auto focus, which can't effectively handle motion, nor can it handle subjects at different distances, nor can it determine what you *want* to have in focus.

The automatic movements of the lens are relatively slow. If the subject is moving around quickly, the auto focus won't be able to keep up with it. You'll end up with an image that is constantly shifting in

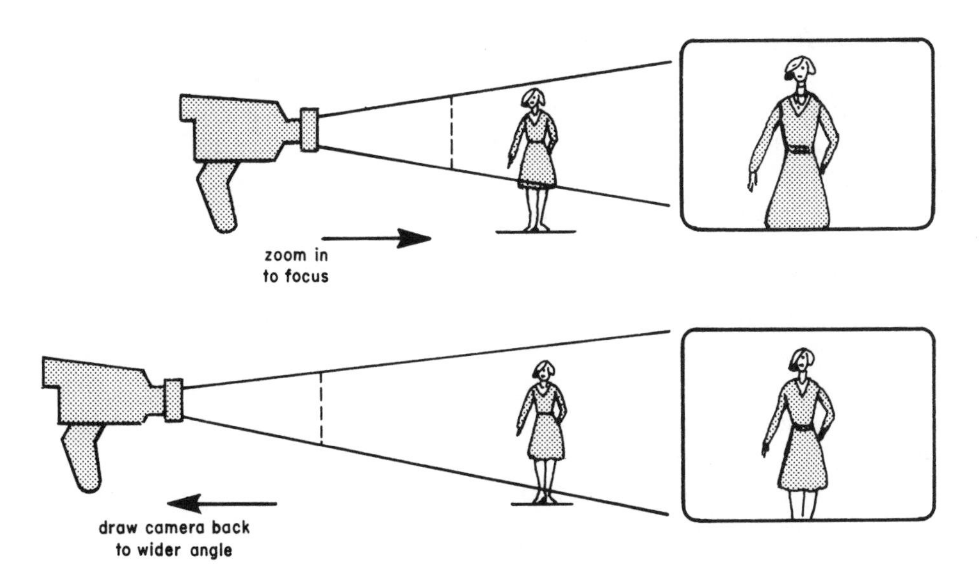

FIG. 5–4 Zoom in to focus; then bring the camera back to the wider angle you wish to use.

and out of focus, mostly by chance. Panning—following the subject in a smooth arc—can partially solve the problem. Better still, set the focus manually, or use the auto focus to set the focus, then lock it in by switching to manual. You can also place yourself at a sufficient distance, use a wide angle and enough light so that the depth-of-field is deep enough to keep a greater range in sharp focus.

Objects in front and in back of each other are a problem. If the camera is focusing on one dominant object 5 feet from the camera, an object 10 feet away is likely to be out of focus. If you want the distant object to be the more important one, the camera won't know. For example, you may want to shoot a picnic with 10 or 20 people; if you're taping through a filmy piece of glass or a chain-link fence, the camera may assume that what you really want to record are the spots on the glass or the fencing. You could end up with blurry people behind clear, sharp water spots or strands of metal.

A continuous variation in distance, such as shooting along a wall or through a large group of people, can cause an even worse problem. The center of focus to the camera doesn't exist in such a case. It picks the happiest medium it can find, depending on how you have aimed the camera, and throws everything else out of focus.

Most auto focusing circuits use infrared or some other invisible signal. The signal is projected from the camera, reflects off the object, comes back to the camera almost instantly, and activates the focusing circuits. (A few circuits use sound, but these are slower; infrared is considerably more efficient.)

You should be aware, however, that some objects don't reflect infrared back to the focusing circuits. Anything black, for example, tends to absorb all light. Water will also absorb infrared, as will certain kinds of glass and fabric; in these cases, the auto focus cannot work accurately. Another common problem is highly reflective objects, such as shiny metal. The "hot spots" of the object will give the auto focus trouble.

Macro Features

The normal range of focus for most home video cameras is from about 3 feet to infinity. Anything closer to the camera than 3 feet will be out of focus, unless you use a macro feature. This allows the lens to function as a close-up lens, with a range of, perhaps, 1 inch to 1 foot (see Fig. 2–15).

Focus is critical when using the macro feature. In the normal mode, the depth-of-field of the lens under a certain lighting condition might be between 4 and 10 feet. While in macro under those same conditions, the range of focus might be between 2 and 3 inches: anything outside this range is likely to be so far out of focus as to be unrecognizable.

Use of a tripod to steady the camera is essential. Normal body "sway" of a half-inch or so won't be noticeable when you're shooting a football game from 50 feet away. It will be terrible when you're shooting just inches away. A half-inch of movement from 50 feet is a ratio of 1:1200. That same movement from 3 inches away is a ratio of 1:6. To get that same effect at the football game, the camera would have to be moving about 8 feet forward and backward, or side-to-side, as though swinging on a pendulum.

If your camera doesn't have a macro feature, you can buy an accessory lens for close-ups. The same rules apply: focus carefully and use a tripod.

Telephoto, Wide-Angle, and Zoom Lenses

There are characteristics specific to the focal length of a lens. A wide-angle (or short) lens takes in more of a scene due to its wider angle of coverage. It has a greater depth-of-field, and the tendency to optically bend lines and cause distortion.

A telephoto lens takes in less of a scene, while magnifying what it does "see." It has a shallower depth-of-field, putting less of the scene in sharp focus. It also flattens the perspective, making objects seem to be closer together. A building 100 feet in the background may seem in the recording to be only 20 feet away.

The extent of these effects depends on how long or short the lens is. A moderately wide-angle lens will display fewer of these characteristics than a lens that is very wide. For example, a lens that picks up 120 degrees of angle will show those characteristics to a lesser extent than one that picks up 170 degrees of angle. The narrower the angle, the closer those characteristics become to a telephoto, which then increases in that set of characteristics as the angle continues to narrow and the magnification increases.

Most home video cameras come with a lens that moves from being a fair wide angle to a fair telephoto, in a ratio of about 6:1. Many amateurs tend to overuse the telephoto side, and then wonder why everything in the scene seems scrunched and out of focus. If your goal is to bring something at a distance closer, zoom in so that the lens becomes a telephoto. When you do this, expect focus to become more critical, and also expect the perspective of distance to disappear.

The vast majority of home video cameras have power zoom, which makes it possible to zoom in or out with the push of a button—almost always conveniently located so that the operating hand can activate it (Fig. 5–5). While this is the proper way to design a piece of equipment, it also leads many amateurs to overuse the zoom. The recording ends up being in constant motion. Keep in mind the function and effect of the zoom and use it sparingly.

FIG. 5–5 Slide your hand up through the strap, using first and second fingers to operate the zoom.

PANNING

There are two basic reasons for panning. One is because the subject is in motion and you have to move the camera to keep the subject in the frame. The second is when you want to capture a panorama—a wider background than can be captured from a single position. In either case, the trick is to pan slowly and smoothly.

If you're shooting someone who is running across the yard, follow along at the same pace. Generally the idea is to keep the subject in the center of the frame. If the movement is so fast that the background blurs, it is usually an advantage to move back farther so that the panning can be done more slowly. (Keep in mind that panning of any kind can be irritating if overused. It is often more effective to allow the subject to move into, through, and then out of the frame.)

Or perhaps you're trying to capture the beauty of the Grand Canyon. No matter where you stand, you won't be able to see all of it at one time—not with your eyes and not with the camera. By slowly panning from the far left to the far right, the viewers can see the entire

FIG. 5–6 Using two hands and pressing your face against the camera helps to steady it, especially when panning.

scene, just as if they were standing there and turning, taking in the entire scene a little at a time.

There are times when you'll have little choice but to pan while holding the camera, but it is almost always better to take an extra minute to mount it on a tripod. This will help to keep the movement steady, without wobbles or jerks. Another wise investment is one of the straps or brackets that holds the camera tightly against your body. This isn't as steady as a tripod, but is still better than trying to hold the camera by itself, and will give you the mobility you might want or need.

Lacking a tripod, at least brace your body against a wall, tree or fence. It also helps to keep both hands on the camera, and to press the camera against your head (Fig. 5–6).

EMBEDDING TIME, DATE, AND OTHER INFORMATION

Some cameras have the capability to generate and embed the time and date, a handy way to permanently record on the tape when something was shot. If your camera doesn't have a built-in feature, you can write the time, date, and other information on a piece of paper or cardboard and videograph it. You can get even fancier and use a clapboard.

Normally, this information will appear at the beginning of a sequence for only a few seconds. One exception could be when you're trying to tag an event while it's happening. For New Year's Eve, the time and date could both move forward as midnight approaches, then change to note the arrival of the new year. With a little imagination, you can come up with all sorts of ways to sneak in important information without it seeming to be contrived.

Embedding information can serve to help in editing as well. Even putting the lens cap on and recording a few seconds of black can signal you that the scene is about to change, giving you time to pause the VCR, switch tapes, or whatever.

ASPECT RATIO AND COMPOSITION

If you don't like the horizontal composition of a scene, you can turn a still camera on its side and use a vertical format. But a video camera conforms to the standard 3:4 ratio television format. You *can* tilt a video camera safely, or even hold it upside down, but the image will also be tilted or upside-down. Learn to think in terms of the television format, unless you like the idea of also turning your TV on its side for those vertical scenes.

A friend of mine is a professional photographer, and a very good one. When he got his first home video camera, his training had him composing his shots the same way he'd handle composition with his still cameras. His first tape showed beautifully clear scenes and people tipped on their sides—and other scenes that were poorly composed because he was used to cropping and making adjustments in the darkroom.

The ratio of any TV screen is 3:4 (3:5 in high resolution systems). This is called the *aspect ratio.* The viewfinder, pickup, and television screen are all the same. (This obviously doesn't apply in the same way to the "square format" monitors or televisions.) Everything you shoot will be based around this ratio, and with a horizontal alignment. The image will be 3 units high and 4 units long (Fig. 5–7).

The amateur will let the camera do all the work. Since the viewfinder has the same aspect ratio as the pickup, which has the same aspect ratio as the television, it's easy to let the camera do the job of framing. The professional will preview a scene, with a mental image of how things will look before the record button is pushed.

The scene you are videographing has to work within that preset frame, and its composition must create the effect you want. Sometimes this is as simple as making sure that everything important is in the frame; at other times, it involves more complex planning.

FIG. 5–7 Keep the aspect ratio in mind. A standard video pickup and standard TV screen are 4 units wide and 3 units high. You *can't* tip the camera sideways, and if you're too close, your subject will be cut off.

The amateur basically aims and shoots. The ease of editing the recorded tape often makes the situation worse. After all, if the taping doesn't come out completely right, you can easily cut out any bad parts, or even reshoot everything without having to pay anything extra.

The professional will look at the scene, including the back-

FIG. 5–7 *continued.*

ground, before ever starting to shoot. Editing is easy, but it's even easier to do the job right the first time. He also knows that there are too many one-time shots that can never be done over again.

GETTING QUALITY AUDIO

Many people pay close attention to the video, and forget the audio portion. Some may even forget it to the point that they carry on a conversation with someone standing next to them, and then wonder later why they didn't capture the kids talking out in the yard.

Paying attention to the audio becomes even more important when the only microphone being used is mounted on the camera. Regardless, always keep in mind that sounds closest to the microphone will be louder than those sounds coming from farther away. If you're talking while using an on-camera microphone, your own voice will tend to dominate.

Distance, Equipment, and Common Sense

Just as distance will cause the image to lose detail, distance will cause loss of audio. The trick is to get up close to the subject, which not only improves sound quality, but also helps to reduce ambient sound (which exists whether you want it there or not). You could be taping your child outside with his wagon. By getting close, you can reduce or even eliminate the sounds of other children playing. Then, just when he begins to talk, an airplane flies overhead, possibly ruining the audio portion of the recording. The automatic gain control (AGC) can make matters even worse. This circuit is wonderful to have, but it can be a disadvantage since it will automatically try to boost all sound, which includes unwanted noise. Getting close will help to reduce this noise.

You can further control the sound and noise by intelligent use of microphones and other audio equipment.

It begins with a basic microphone choice—directional or omnidirectional (Fig. 5–8). Without exception, the microphone that comes with the home video camera is omnidirectional. This means that it theoretically picks up sound equally well in all directions. For general purposes, this is usually the best choice.

A directional microphone has a narrower angle of pickup. In essence, the directional microphone is aimed. The advantage is that sounds coming from outside the angle of pickup are ignored, or minimal.

You can even combine microphones. You might wish to have microphones located in more than one place. The way to handle this is through the use of an audio mixer. This unit combines (mixes) multiple audio inputs into a single audio output. Usually it will have gain controls for each channel (one channel per microphone), which allows you to balance the microphones, and also to fade them in or out.

When using a mixer, it's important to use the same kind of microphone—even the same brand—throughout. Each type of microphone (omnidirectional or directional) has certain characteristics that go beyond the angle of pickup. The mismatch of characteristics and tonal quality can show up in the recording, giving the final audio an uneven quality.

FIG. 5–8 Microphone pickup patterns.

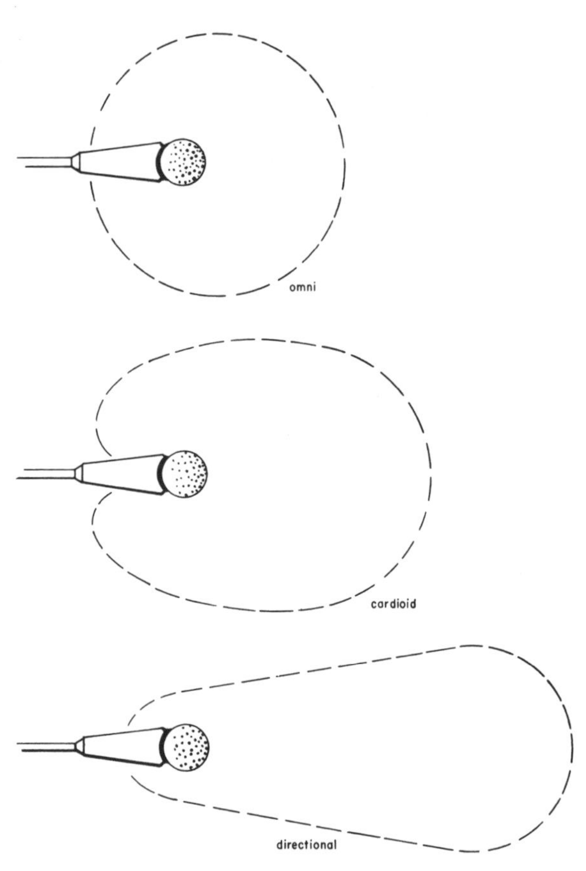

FIG. 5–9 Realistic's stereo audio mixer.

When placing microphones, it is often best to hide them. Not only do the people being recorded feel more relaxed (less "mike fright"), but a hidden microphone is not so distracting for the viewer. Whenever possible, avoid flat or hard surfaces. Even when the microphone isn't actually touching the surface, sound reflections add a strange and displeasing quality. If the microphone *is* touching a hard surface, any vibration in the area is more likely to be picked up as an irritating noise.

Audio Dubbing

Sometimes a video can be greatly improved by dubbing in a different audio track. Most home decks are not capable of sound-on-sound (adding audio while leaving the existing audio in place). Many can't even perform sound-over-sound (replacing the audio while leaving the video intact). Look at your VTR and see if it has an "Audio Dub" feature. If it does, you can replace the existing sound track with another.

If your VTR doesn't have this capability, and if you don't have access to equipment capable of audio dub, you'll either have to do the audio dub while dubbing the video or forget replacing the audio.

Both the playback and recording decks have video and audio jacks. For normal dubbing, you'd connect the outputs of the playback deck to the inputs of the recording deck (Fig. 5–10). To substitute other audio, you merely connect that other audio source to the audio input of the recording deck and leave the audio output of the playback deck dangling. (You could also run both audio signals through a mixer, but this goes back into the realm of professional equipment.)

Technically, it's illegal to use someone else's music or sound track. Whether you violate copyright law or not depends on the use of the end result: if it's commercial, you've broken a federal law.

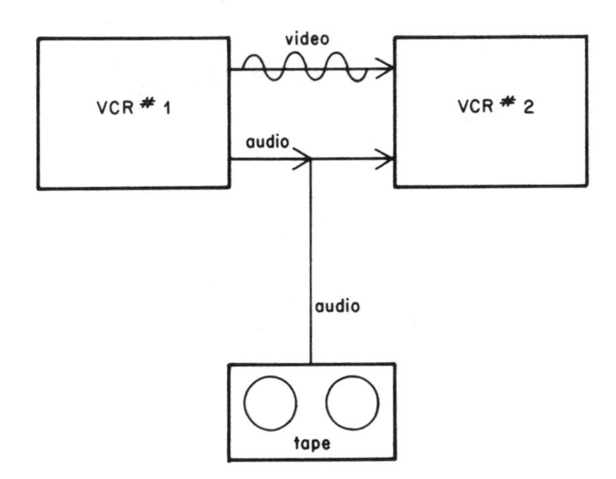

FIG. 5–10 Adding audio to the existing audio, or merging audio tracks.

TIPS ON VIDEOGRAPHY

The amateur videographer will rely exclusively on the viewfinder. This greatly limits the field of view, which in turn can cause you to miss important events just out of the camera's range. With a little practice, you'll have a good idea of what the camera is seeing and recording. By looking over the top of the viewfinder instead of through it, you'll have a much broader field of view and will be able to see things about to move into the frame or events important enough so that you'll want to swing the camera over to capture them.

Even more effective is learning to shoot with both eyes open. Again, you will improve your peripheral view, while still being able to see what is happening through the viewfinder. This takes a little practice. One eye will be seeing the miniature b&w image and, thus, what the camera is seeing. Meanwhile your other eye will be seeing the scene as it really is, and beyond the edges of the camera's view.

Preplanning and in-camera editing (see Chapters 7 and 8) will help you to record the important events and eliminate what you don't want. Depending on the complexity of your taping, this can be as sim-

FIG. 5–11 A storyboard doesn't have to be complicated if you plan to ad lib dialogue, but you need one so everyone knows what to do next.

ple as the action of your thumb on the on/off button, or as detailed as making up a storyboard so your cast of characters knows what will happen—and when.

Preplanning can help you to avoid short bursts. A scene of only 4 or 5 seconds is there and gone before the viewers can become a part of it. Flashing tiny bits of a number of scenes might be useful at times, as a special effect, but if you do it all the time your tape will be unwatchable. A basic rule of thumb is to keep the camera recording for a minimum of 10 to 15 seconds, and then mix these shorter clips with longer ones. Very long scenes can be just as bad. Watching a new baby playing on the lawn is wonderful. A tiny 3-second burst of the baby isn't enough. Watching 3 hours of the baby picking at blades of grass will bore even the grandparents!

Chapter 6

Lighting: Illumination, Composition, Mood

Photography and videography are the capturing of light, particularly reflected light. Without proper light, you won't be able to capture an image. The single most important element of a decent video recording (followed closely by the audio), good lighting makes the difference between a video that looks professional and one that looks like your 3-year-old nephew got his hands on the camera.

The three basic functions of lighting are illumination, composition, and mood. All three are closely linked and work as three parts of the whole. There are no clear-cut division lines where one leaves off and another begins. Obviously, you can't compose a scene without illumination. Less obvious to the amateur is that you can't illuminate without causing both a certain composition and a certain mood.

Illumination is the amount of light needed to allow the scene to be recorded properly. It is determined by the sensitivity of the camera you are using; the less sensitive the camera, the more light you'll need for proper illumination.

Composition is how the scene looks, including which areas are bright and which are dim. Brightly lit portions are dominant, while subjects in the shadows tend to appear less important. The way lights are positioned, and thus the arrangement of illumination, determines how the scene is composed. Having three 100-watt floods aimed straight at a subject will give plenty of illumination. So will directing those same three lights from different angles—but the composition and mood of each will be different.

Mood is the overall effect of your scene. While someone standing in the shadows during a newscast seems irrelevant, that same person in a mystery movie creates a sense of tension. The scene is illuminated and composed to create the mood you want, whether a formal, brightly and evenly lighted scene where everything is of equal importance, or a high-contrast set with brightly lighted areas and deep shadows.

Many other factors come into play. Most are integral parts of the three overall functions. The color of the light, for example, can make a great difference in the end recording. Red lights will produce a warm scene. A blue light can be used to simulate the moon. But it's more complex than merely adding a colored light: the nature of light and lamps must be taken into consideration (see Chapter 5, "Using Light and Color to Advantage").

The differences between the camera and the human eye may make for surprises: a striped jacket may look fine to you, but creates video interference. Certain fabrics look dark blue to your eye, but appear glowing reddish-purple in the video replay.

As you read this chapter, keep in mind that everything is interrelated. You can't have composition without illumination, and illumination will cause both composition and mood, whether you want it to or not. The trick is to control the lighting so that you control its features and effects.

QUANTITY OF LIGHT

In order to record a scene, there must be enough light for the camera to "see" what it's shooting. This is oversimplified and, unfortunately, is also where many amateurs stop, flooding the scene with light—period.

Too little light will cause the image to be grainy, probably with a greenish cast. As you continue to add light, the scene becomes brighter and the colors more true. Eventually, you'll reach a point where the scene—or parts of it—are too bright and become washed out. It's even possible that the camera, and especially one with a tube pickup, will be damaged.

The power consumption of a lamp is rated in watts. (See "Power Consumption" later in this chapter.) The amount of light it puts out is rated in lumens and foot-candles, the second being the measurement that concerns the photographer and videographer. A foot-candle is the amount of light across a surface of 1 square foot coming from a standard candle at a distance of 1 foot (Fig. 6–1). One hundred such candles at the same distance on the same surface is 100 foot-candles, as would be a lamp that glows as brightly as those 100 candles.

If you move that candle back, the Inverse Square Law of lighting comes into play (Fig. 6–2). The distance from light source to subject in this example is twice as great. The amount of light falling on the subject is one-fourth. (Inverse of 2 is ½. The square of the inverse is ¼.) The same applies to the 100 foot-candle source. Double the distance from source to subject, and you'll get ¼ the light, or 25 foot-candles.

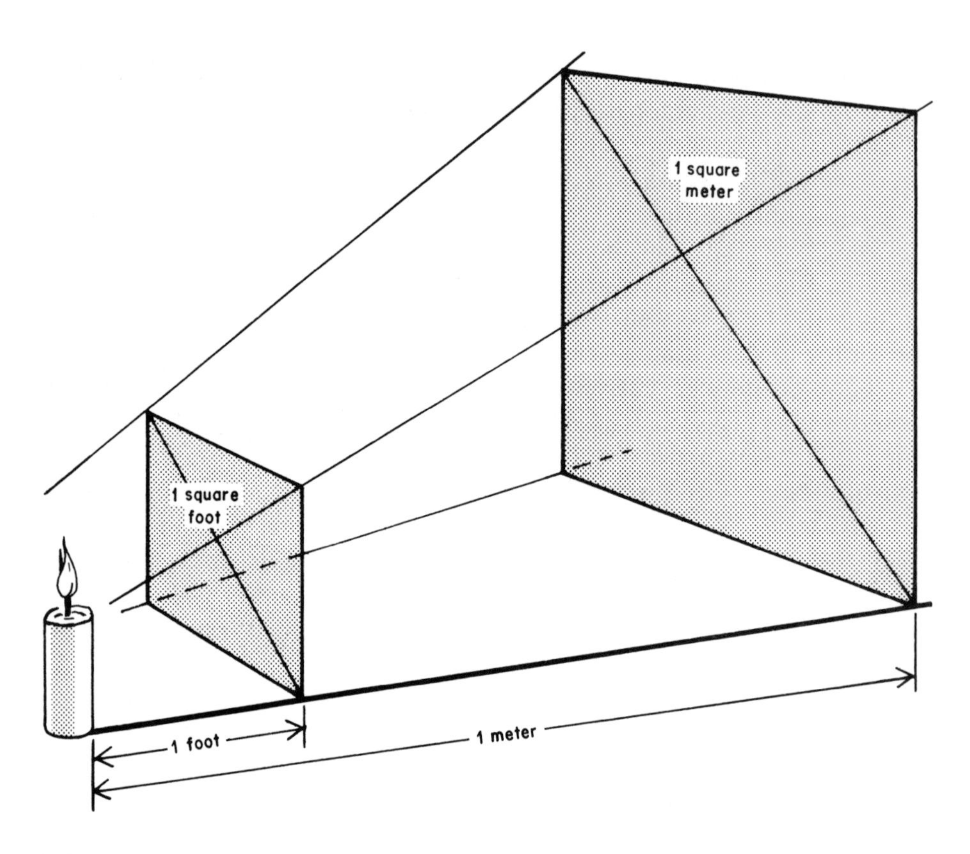

FIG. 6–1 A *foot-candle* is the amount of light from a standard candle across a surface of one square foot from a distance of one foot. A *meter-candle* is calculated the same way.

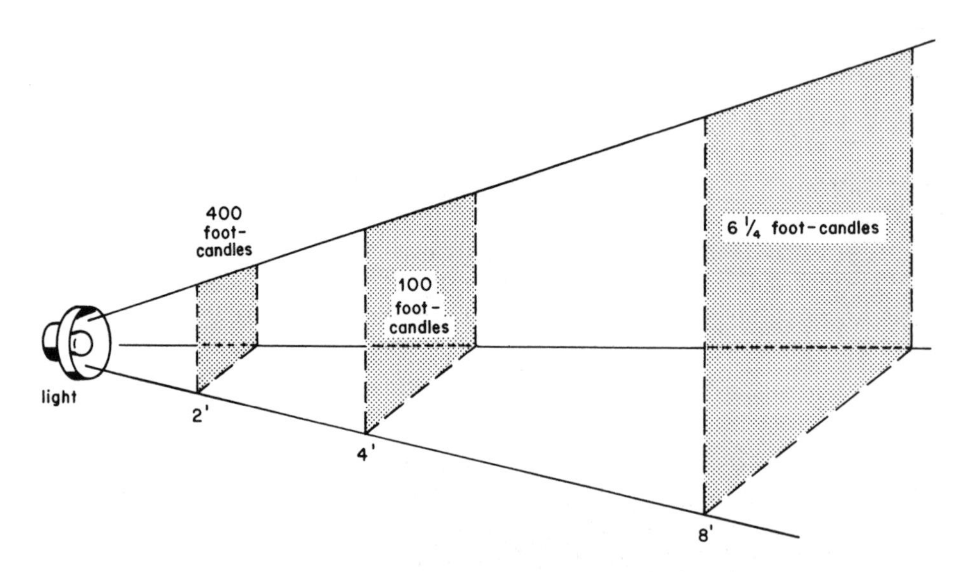

FIG. 6–2 The Inverse Square Law: the amount of light falling on the subject decreases from the original amount by the square of the increased distance.

Double the distance again, to 8 feet, and the amount of light falling on the subject drops to just $\frac{1}{16}$th its original intensity, or about 6¼ foot-candles.

This relates directly to the video camera's sensitivity rating. Lux is the metric unit of measurement, equal to the light of that same standard candle across a surface of 1 square meter from a distance of 1 meter (Fig. 6–1). As you can see from the Inverse Square Law, 1 lux is considerably less bright than 1 foot-candle. In fact, it is $\frac{1}{10}$th as bright (so that 10 lux is about equal to 1 foot-candle).

Modern video cameras boast a sensitivity of 10 lux or better, but that doesn't mean that you'll get a good recording. At 10 lux, the scene is likely to be dim, grainy, and have a greenish cast. The 10 lux rating is a minimum. Even the best cameras require considerably more light to record the image decently. Even 100 lux (10 foot-candles) may not be enough to provide a good recording with true colors. The instruction manual with your camera probably suggests using a *minimum* of 500 lux. (Full sunlight is as much as 100,000 lux, or 10,000 foot-candles.)

Professionals often use a light meter to determine if the scene will be sufficiently illuminated to create a quality recording. Remember that you can't rely on the human eye, because it's so sensitive and so adaptable that a scene will look just fine to you, while badly under-illuminated for the video camera. (On a clear night, the stars, plus the city skyline, might seem bright to your eye. The home video camera probably won't even "see" them.) If you don't have a videographer's light meter—one that measures either foot-candles or lux—experience is a fair substitute. But expect to make mistakes and end up with some scenes of relatively poor quality.

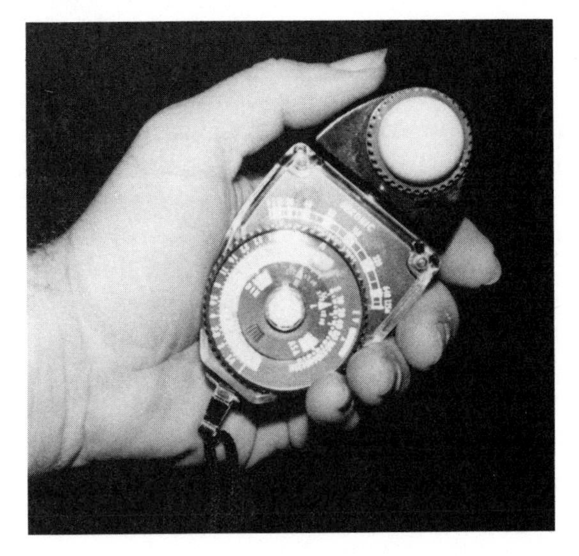

FIG. 6–3 Using a light meter.

QUALITY OF LIGHT

Types of Illumination and How They Differ

So-called "natural light" is most commonly thought of as being from the sun. It has the advantage of being plentiful and free. It also changes. Morning and evening sunlight comes in at a sharper angle. Because it passes through more atmosphere, it is less intense and has a redder color (as far as the camera is concerned). As noon approaches, the sunlight is much more intense and also becomes more and more blue (again, as far as the camera is concerned). Indirect sunlight, such as that scattered by cloud cover or in the shade, is always more blue than open sunlight. Throughout the range, the video camera can adjust rather easily. Even so, a scene with both open sunlight and shade can cause problems. Either the sunlit portions will appear reddish, or the shadows will seem blue.

Just how you set the white balance depends a lot on circumstances. Will you be shooting primarily in open sunlight? Will most of the action be in the shady areas? Will there be time to reset the camera for the dominant portions of the scene as it moves. (Keep in mind that open areas are likely to the "washed out" when the camera is set for proper exposure of the shaded areas.)

With incandescent lamps, you have more control. Artificial lighting is generally your only choice when shooting at night and often when shooting inside. While the sun changes in color and intensity from dawn to dusk, and from one type of weather or climate to another, incandescent lighting changes relatively little.

In an incandescent bulb, electricity flows through a filament, causing it to heat. The hot wire then gives off light. The filament is tungsten because it doesn't burn up as fast as other materials. The bulb is filled with a mixture of nitrogen and argon to about 0.8 atmospheres. This helps to keep the filament from boiling away. It still evaporates, becomes thinner over time, and finally burns out. The hotter the lamp, the shorter the life. And the more powerful the lamp, the hotter it tends to run. Just as bad for photographers and videographers is the loss of illumination intensity and a decrease in the color temperature due to black deposits of the tungsten on the lamp glass.

In a halogen lamp, the halogen begins a cycle by which the boiled-off tungsten is put back on the filament instead of on the glass of the bulb. For this cycle to work, a temperature of 600°C is best; if the bulb glass temperature goes below 250°C, the cycle stops and tungsten is deposited on the glass. This cycle is the reason that the amount of light given off by a halogen lamp stays constant throughout its life at the same color temperature. The seal area must not exceed 350°C to 450°C (depending on life expectancy of the lamp). There is a foil seal of molybdenum that can oxidize. Special design is needed especially around the seal and socket.

A halogen lamp by its nature tends to get very hot. Some people have thought to increase safety by installing fans to blow air over the lamps, but this defeats the purpose of using halogen lamps. As heat increases on the filament, the color temperature goes up. Bulbs designed to simulate the color temperature of sunlight tend to be extremely hot and consequently have a relatively short lifespan.

A second means of simulating the color temperature of sunlight is to use a blue filter. Many daylight bulbs have blue glass for the envelope. Another method is to place a blue gel in front of the lamp. In both cases, since much of the red end of the color spectrum is being absorbed, a lot of heat is generated. Cheap gels will often melt. Bulbs with blue glass will also become very hot, which in turn shortens the life of the bulb.

Measuring Color Temperature

In stage theater and for some films, colored lights are used to create effects and moods. A blue light on a dark stage, for example, simulates a scene lighted by the moon.

The same thing can be done with video, although greater care is needed because of the white balance of the video camera. For a red light to videograph red, the white balance must be adjusted and locked on white light. All you need is a white light and a white card or someone wearing a white shirt. Aim the camera at this white surface, then adjust and lock the white balance. (If the video camera is set to auto white, the camera will attempt to adjust itself as though the red light were actually white.) You can see how the quality of light color creates composition and mood for a specific effect.

The color temperature of light is determined by the temperature of a perfect black body, heated to provide a certain color. At absolute zero, the object would give off no energy. As it becomes hotter, it gives off more and more energy. The temperature is rated in degrees Kelvin (K). Heated to 3200°K, the object glows with a light equivalent in color to a studio photo flood. At about 5500°K, the color temperature is about the same as sunlight. This is theoretical; it has little to do with actual *heat* as we normally think of it.

The light of a candle is about 1900°K; incandescent lamps are 3200°K; sunlight is about 5500°K; as the numbers increase, the light becomes redder. Despite the incredible ability of your eyes to adjust across the range, you *can* see a difference: light a room with incandescent lamps, then look outside. The inside will have a warmer look to it. The shade outside will seem slightly blue in comparison. These differences are seen to a much greater extent by the camera.

Keep this in mind when illuminating a scene. If your intention is to use colored light for a particular effect, fine. Do so purposely, not by accidentally mixing the sources of light.

SELECTIVE COMPOSITION

Light can be controlled, just like a piece of scenery or a prop, to "paint" a scene.

When you look at a scene, you will pick out the parts that are most important to you. A number of little details will go unnoticed, but the camera will pick up everything, including cruel details, unless the lighting is designed to disguise or hide them.

What do you want the viewer to see? And to not see? The idea is to use selective illumination to compose the scene.

In essence, composition begins by determining what is most important and what to exclude. Important parts of a scene are generally well and evenly lighted. Less important areas are usually placed off in the shadows, purposely underplayed. This means that the best way to begin is to mentally preview the scene. Position the important subjects and then position the lights so that these subjects are well lighted. (See "Physical Lighting Setups" later in this chapter.)

You may not think that you have much control over the lighting outside. While it's true that you can't reach up and move the sun, you still have a variety of choices. One of the easiest is to pick the right time of day so that the natural lighting is doing what you want it to do. Professional videographers sometimes call the first hour after sunrise and the last hour before sunset "the golden hours." The sun is somewhat softer and warmer, and shadows aren't as deep, although they are longer, Toward noon, the light becomes more harsh. Shadows become smaller but darker. On a cloudy day, shadows will be extremely soft, or even nonexistent.

Positioning your subjects can also go a long way toward composing a successful scene. Don't let half the scene be in full sun while the other half is in the shade (Fig. 6–4). Reposition the subjects, the camera, or both. Don't forget the physical composition of the shot. Remove trash bags and other distracting items. Position the subjects so that the background complements the scene, rather than causing interference.

Reflector boards can be used to throw sunlight into the shadows. For softer "fill" light, a white board is used. For a spotlight effect, use a board with a surface of crinkled metal foil.

The only artificial lights suitable for use along with sunlight are lamps with a color temperature of at least 5000°K, called "daylight" lamps. Artificial lights are easier to control when composing a critical scene where you are after a certain effect or mood.

FIG. 6–4 Trash bags and other unwanted objects not only make the physical composition sloppy, but also interfere with the lighting. Note the peculiar shadow cast across the person at right; you want to eliminate the source before you shoot.

CREATING MOOD

Creating a mood with lighting can be simple or complex. One light aimed straight into a scene is basic illumination. The mood is then set by the intensity of that light (as well as by such elements as costuming, action, dialogue). Now move that single light so that there are hard shadows. The scene becomes more dramatic. Move it near the floor so that it shines upward and across the subject's face. Scary!

Vary mood by varying the number of lights. The intensity of light. The direction, the color, the softness or hardness, the props around the lights. . .

With a little imagination and experimentation, you can create a wide variety of moods using only two or three lights. Combine lighting with other elements. Take bright and even lighting as an example: with an ordinary scene, the mood is friendly; change the background and costuming to dominant whites and the mood becomes sterile and

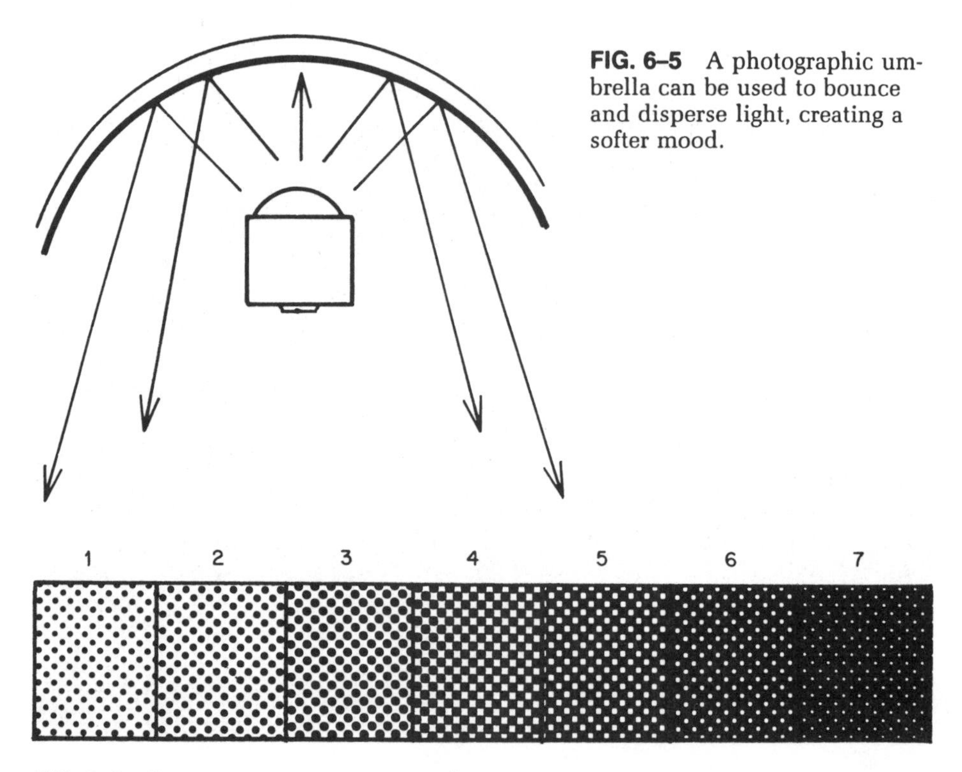

FIG. 6–5 A photographic umbrella can be used to bounce and disperse light, creating a softer mood.

FIG. 6–6 Seven-step contrast grey scale.

futurisitic; change to a black background, and the effect is somewhat bizarre.

Using bounced (reflected) and diffuse lighting lends softness to a scene. Taken to an extreme, it can make things appear dreamy. Less light with harsher shadows (changing the lighting angle) can be used to create an ominous mood. The moods created can be highly dramatic or subtle. For home videos, creating mood may not seem important, and in many cases it's not. Even then, however, an awareness of the emotional effect of different kinds of lighting can help prevent the accidental creation of moods you *don't* want.

PHYSICAL LIGHTING SETUPS

Lighting schemes carry out all three functions: primary, of course, is to illuminate the scene; a close second is the positioning of the lights to compose the scene as you wish it to appear; third is the mood that is created.

A still photographer usually thinks of lighting as being one light, two lights, three lights. The videogapher is often dealing with motion and/or a larger area. Professional videographers use what is called *the point system*. Instead of thinking of the number of lights, they think of the number of directions from which light is coming.

The light in *one-point lighting* is most commonly coming from the front. It could be from a single lamp, or from a spread-out bank of lights across the front of a stage. There could easily be 10 or more lights used, but it is still one-point lighting, since all light is coming from the same direction.

With rare exception, the first light or set of lights handles the bulk of the work. It provides the basic illumination needed in the scene and makes it bright enough for the camera. The second and third points should complement the primary and complete the "painting" of the scene.

Exactly how you arrange the lights depends on your needs and on the lighting equipment you have available. If you have just one lamp and nothing else, you'll have little choice but to confine yourself to one-point lighting. Add a second lamp or a reflector board and you can take advantage of two-point lighting or more expanded one-point lighting.

One-Point Lighting

The first light is the *key* light. In one-point lighting, it is doing all the work. It tends to cast harsh shadows. Your goal is to make it even

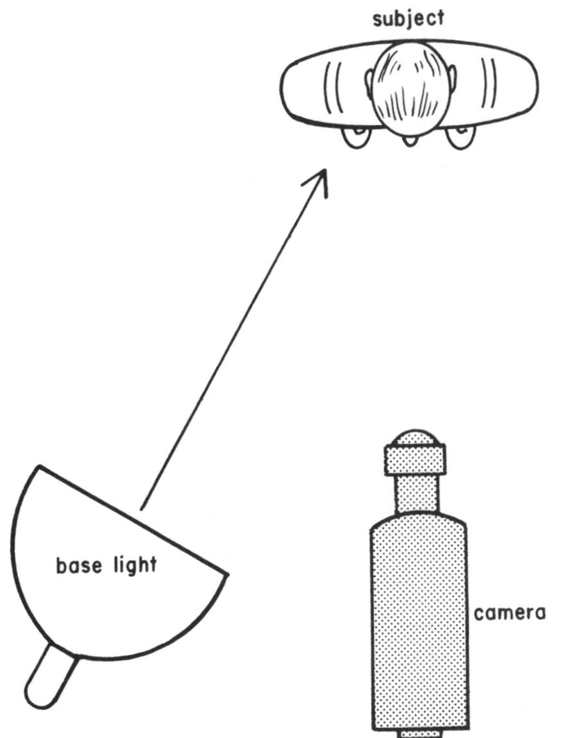

FIG. 6–7 Single-light setup.

across the subject and try to avoid harsh shadows. This is commonly done by shining the light at an angle. You might want to move it off to the side, raise it, or both. Normally an angle of 45° is the maximum. More than this can cause some odd effects, and even 45° is too great an angle for many subjects, causing unsightly shadows. One-point lighting can be used to emphasize form, texture, or mood, depending on your needs (see Figs. 6–7 through 6–14).

FIG. 6–8 Inadequate lighting produces shadows on the image and too little definition against the background.

FIG. 6–9 Using a reflector card to direct light onto subject from a different direction without adding lights.

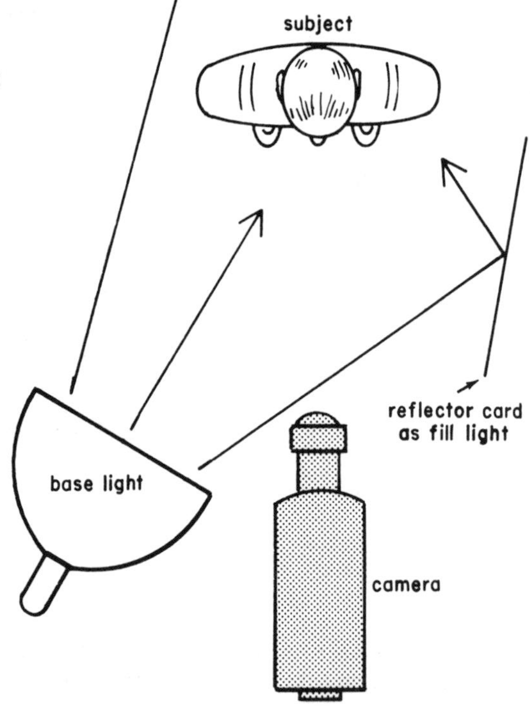

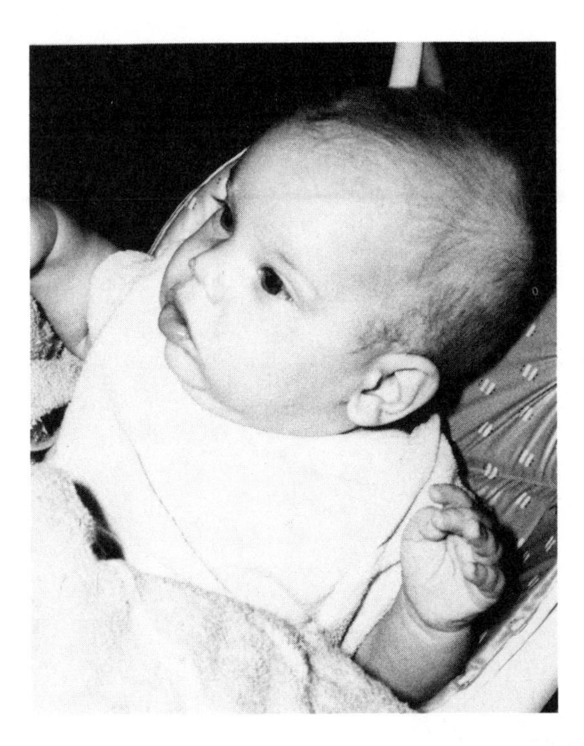

FIG. 6–10 A single light will often make the subject appear flat, or washed out.

FIG. 6–11 One-point lighting also tends to cast harsh shadows.

FIG. 6–12 Setting the light at an angle can make lighting more pleasing; too extreme an angle, however, will cause strange shadows (perfect if you *want* this sinister effect).

FIG. 6–13 Here, the light has been raised to the proper angle, making the shot more pleasing.

FIG. 6–14 The effects of a single light from the front and from the side.

Two-Point Lighting

Two-point lighting begins with placement of the key light to provide basic illumination of the scene and subjects. The second light is then most commonly set to do one of two things. It can be used as a fill or it can be positioned as a back light. Both do just what their names imply.

A *fill light* fills in the shadows, softening them so that they are less harsh and more pleasing. Some shadowing is needed to give dimension and depth (Fig. 6–16).

"Classical" lighting has the balance between the key light and fill light approximately 1.5:1, the key light being roughly half again as bright as the fill. Both lights are set to come in at an angle; angles are determined by the subject, and the composition, and the mood desired.

A back light is used to separate subject from the background and to add dimension and shape. It shines on the subject from behind and provides depth. When back lighting a person, placement is usually fairly high so that the light strikes the hair and shoulders from above.

A back light and a background light are not the same. A back light shines on the subject from the back, while a background light shines on the background. You will use a background light with a two-light setup only rarely, but there are times when using the second light on the background will emphasize color or important details.

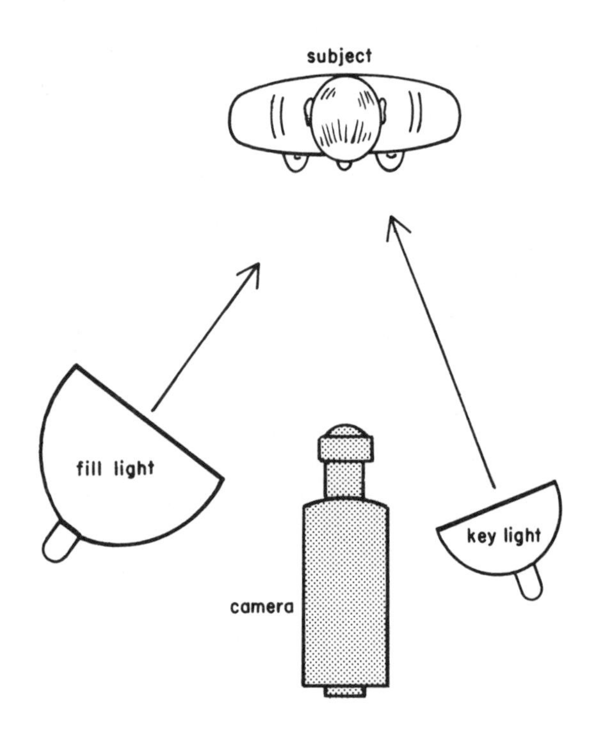

FIG. 6–15 Key and fill light setup.

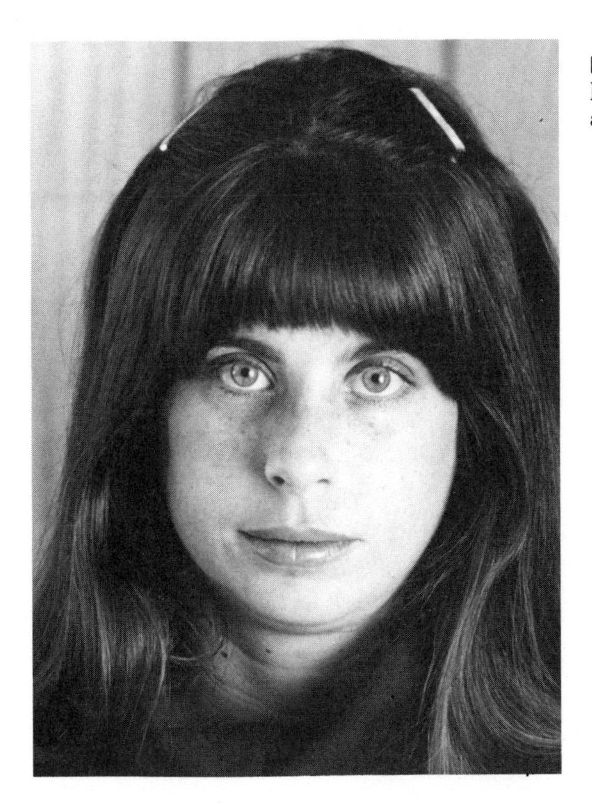

FIG. 6–16 Using key and fill lights helps to soften a picture and add detail.

Three-Point Lighting

Three-point lighting gives you much more control and versatility. Using three lights gets complicated, but this setup tends to be more forgiving. Most commonly, three-point lighting involves a key light, a fill light, and a back light (Fig. 6–17). The key light provides the main illumination; the fill light softens the shadows created by the key light; and the back light separates the subject from the background and adds depth.

Three-point lighting demands that you spend hands-on time experimenting. It's not the sort of thing you can learn entirely from a book, since no one can specify the exact lighting needed for each and every subject and circumstance. For one subject, you may want the key light raised to 6 feet and set off to the side by 30°; for another subject, the key may need to be placed straight on, at a height of 4 feet.

Fill and back lights will be adjusted for the subject, the circumstances, and your goals for form, texture, composition, and mood. In some cases, you'll want the fill light to be 90° opposite the key light, at the same height and with the traditional 1.5:1 intensity ratio. At other times, its best position will be 45° opposite, lower in height than the key, and less intense—perhaps 2:1.

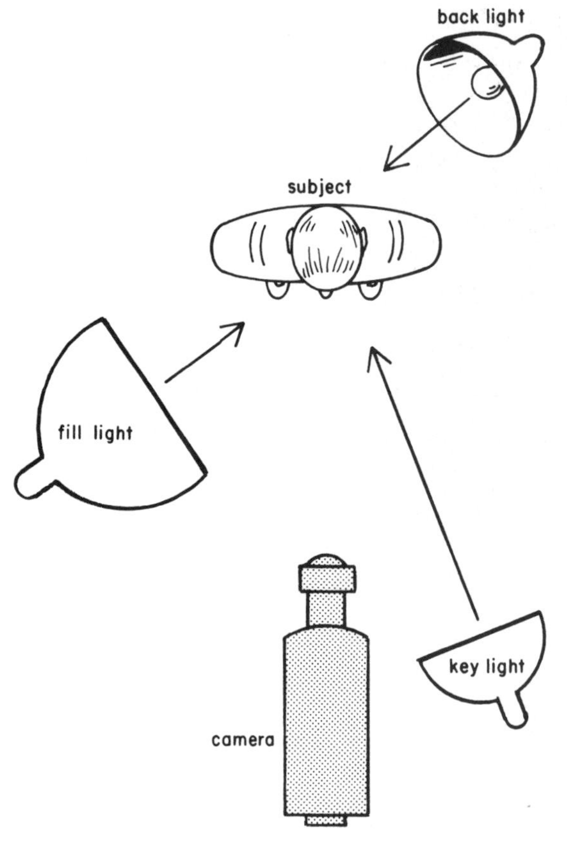

FIG. 6–17 A three-light setup.

FIG. 6–18 Result with back lighting only.

FIG. 6–19 Effect of using key and back lights.

FIG. 6–20 Effect of using fill and background lights.

FIG. 6–21 Three-point lighting, using key, fill, and back lights.

A good starting point is to first set the key light so that it provides the primary illumination. Usually, the goal is to have the subject lighted in such a way that there are distinctive shadows to create the desired form and texture. This light may be moved from side to side, up and down, forward and back.

Once the key light is set, the fill light is placed to soften shadows without casting any new or conflicting shadows. Once again, movement of the light for the correct positioning is side to side, up and down, forward and back. These movements adjust angle and intensity. The idea is to get the fill light to complement the key light. The back light can then be brought into play. Almost always, it will be placed behind and above the subject. It generally requires less moving around than the other lights.

When positioning lights, keep their individual functions in mind, but remember that you want them to work together as a team. How does the scene look? Move the lights, in order—and how does it look now? Does the lighting enhance your concept? Is the subject properly illuminated? Are the proper things highlighted? Do the lighting angles create the textures and moods you want to achieve?

Complex Lighting Setups

There are very few occasions when three-point lighting won't be adequate; usually, adding more lights gets too complicated and may make matters worse. A fourth light may create conflicting shadows, for example, or negate one of the other lights. More complex lighting systems are used to advantage when expanding the area illuminated, where a group of lights some distance off to the side works as a key light.

Otherwise, it's best to avoid anything more complex than three-point lighting on the subject. There are always exceptions, such as when the subject, the camera, or both are moving, or when more than one camera is used to shoot the subject from various angles.

Lighting Action Sequences

A still camera either shoots a subject that isn't moving, or stops the motion of a moving subject. A video camera is meant to record motion, whether simply someone talking to the camera, or a whole football game.

When the action takes place over a large area, lighting it with lamps an be difficult, if not impossible. A 100-watt flood might provide adequate illumination across 20 or 30 feet of width, but even then it drops in intensity toward the edges. Move the light back so that it spreads out better, and you'll get a decrease in intensity (the Inverse Square Law, remember?).

One solution is to tape such things only on nice, sunny days. Then all you have to worry about are shadows and perhaps an occasional cloud. When artificial lighting is required, use multiple lamps, with each lighting a certain portion of the scene and overlapping so that the intensity of the light is even across the entire area.

How to Get Professional Results

Although your eyes are considerably more sensitive and adaptable than the video camera pickup, you can teach yourself to view scenes and to make intelligent guesses as to how good the illumination is. Experimentation and experience are the keys. The more you shoot, the more accurate will be your guesses.

The electronic viewfinder (E/V) of your video camera can help to a certain degree. Once again, experience will guide you. Contrast, in particular, tends to show up well through the b&w viewfinder. Shadows that might go unnoticed on a color monitor will often become apparent through the finder.

Having a color monitor is as important as having a light meter. Small, portable, battery-operated color monitors can be purchased for under $200. (Before you plunk down your money, test the portable TV/monitor for color accuracy. A monitor with poor color is more useless than none at all.) Sometimes the purpose of illumination is to simulate some other effect. A light meter won't be of much help in determining if your "fireplace" *will* look like one in the recording. Nor can you completely trust your eyes, but a check of the monitor should tell you.

Before you begin videographing, ask yourself questions about the scene. How does it look to your eye? Is there enough light on the subjects to see them easily? Are shadows falling where they shouldn't? Are there important parts of the scene with no light, or insufficient light? Conversely, are parts of the scene that you want hidden being blasted with light? If it doesn't look good to your eye, you can bet it's going to look even worse to the video camera.

How does it look to a light meter? Is there enough light for the scene to be recorded? Do you need more light? Where? Where should less light be used? To what extent?

How does it look in the electronic viewfinder, and on a connected color monitor? Has your eye been fooled? And perhaps the meter as well? Is the camera reacting to someone's striped suit? Is your subject blending into the background?

Look for the obvious. If a light-complexioned subject is wearing a white shirt in front of a white background, you're going to have trouble. The subject can disappear into the background. Lighting a situation like this is tricky.

Not quite so obvious are situations where the abilities of your eyes exceed the abilities of the camera. Close stripes of high contrast can cause trouble. Bright or fluorescent colors might look wonderful to your eye, but cause bleeding, flaring, or blooming—one color becoming dominant on the screen, to the point of that color "taking over" objects around it.

You should also be sensitive to contrast: my own front yard is a typical Arizona desert. The land is flat and is essentially the same off into the distance, to a mountain range some 25 miles away that is semi-hidden in a haze. This extremely low-contrast scene can cause trouble. But were I to videotape at the foot of that mountain range right at sunset, heavy shadows would create a high-contrast scene, which can be just as troublesome.

CALCULATING POWER CONSUMPTION

The amount of power consumed by lights is usually of little concern to the home videographer. However, it can become critical if you are using a number of lights.

The standard home electrical circuit is capable of carrying 15 amps. Some are rated at 20 amps, but if you're not positive, then assume that the limit is 15 amps. The basic power formula is $P = IE$, which means that the amount of power consumed (in watts) is equal to the current (I) times the voltage (E). The nominal voltage in your home is 117. Trouble is, this can vary. In most areas, the voltage will go up or down by 10 volts or more on an average day, and can dip even further during a peak period.

If you are getting 120 volts, that 15 amp circuit can handle 15 × 120, or 1800 watts. If the voltage drops to 110 volts, it can handle only 1650 watts. If you load up a circuit with 1800 watts and the voltage drops, the circuit will be overloaded. (Personally, I like to give myself a margin of safety by assuming that the voltage is 110 at all times.)

The formula can be juggled algebraically to yield $I = P/E$ (current equals wattage divided by voltage) and $E = P/I$ (voltage equals wattage divided by the current). Only $P = IE$ and $I = P/E$ are important here, the second being most valuable when calculating the draw on a circuit from the lamps used.

A single 100-watt lamp draws just slightly less than an amp. Plugging the values into the formula you get $I = 100/110$, or .91 amps rounded off. A 500-watt lamp will draw 500/110, or 4.54 amps. (Three such lamps will bring you very close to the maximum capability of the circuit.)

Most home videographers won't have to worry too much about overloading household circuits, but if you have a few 100-watt lamps on the same circuit as other household appliances, it could casue trouble. Best to either change to another circuit or to wait until those appliances are not in use.

Chapter 7

Composition and Planning

You've probably seen home movies where the only forethought used was to load the camera. Everything plods along from scene to scene and back again, without any order or intelligence. Then the person with the camera somehow gets the idea that zooming in and out is a wonderful way to show how sophisticated the camera is, and that panning is an excellent way to "add excitement" (but only succeeds in creating a need for motion-sickness pills).

Meanwhile, people are placed so that phone poles seem to grow out of their heads. There are some wonderful shots of the sky, but the background is so bright that everything else turns black. The quality of the scenes doesn't improve, but finally you're treated to some cute shots of the kids—only to have the screen go blank.

"Oops. This is where the battery ran out of power."

Composition and preplanning aren't difficult. You don't have to go to school to learn how, nor do you need to write lengthy scripts and have everyone memorize lines. In fact, for a home video of a family picnic or your baby's first birthday, too much preplanning and rehearsing can remove the spontaneity. Nevertheless, the more important the taping, the more important planning becomes.

PREPARATION

Nothing ruins the fun of videography faster or more assuredly than poor preparation. Having a battery go dead or running out of tape can be anything from a minor irritation to a complete disaster, depending on the importance of the shooting. However, if you treat even the most casual shootings as critical, you'll get into the habit of preparation and will never find yourself in a less forgiving circumstance.

A part of preparation is continuous maintenance of the equipment. (Steps for this are in Chapter 10.) Proper care and storage of your equipment will help ensure that it doesn't malfunction at the wrong time. It will also help to keep the equipment organized. A case or bag not only serves to protect the equipment, it gives you a single and convenient place for the peripherals so you don't waste valuable time searching (Fig. 7–1).

The most basic "kit" contains the camera and VTR (or camcorder), the microphone, at least one battery, the battery charger, a monitor, an AC adaptor, an extension cord, at least two cassettes, an RF modulator, 75-ohm to 300-ohm adaptor, and all of the basic cables to connect the camera equipment.

You can add to this as you go along. One of the first purchases should be some kind of lighting kit (see Chapter 6), complete with its own set of cords and cables, and preferably with its own carrying case. Adding some spare bulbs is wise, since these have the unfortunate habit of burning out at just the wrong time. Extra cassettes are cheap, and no one should even consider going to a shoot without at least two. A third and even a fourth guarantees that you'll have plenty of recording time, and a safety margin in case of cassette problems.

Extra battery packs are expensive but well worth the cost. Don't forget to carry spare camera function batteries, should these be required (such as for a clock). It's also highly important to keep rechargeable batteries charged. Even then, bring along the AC adaptor and a long extension cord. Your range will be limited, but you can modify your plans easier to those limits than you can to a dead camera. A nice accessory, although not an essential one, is a 12-volt adaptor that allows you to operate the camera from the cigarette lighter in your car. Be sure to carry extra heavy-gauge extension cords: the longer the cord, the heavier the wire should be.

✔

Basic Videography Kit	**Additional Items**
Camera and VTR (or camcorder)	Lights and stands (3)
Microphone	Tripod
Battery	Spare bulbs
Battery charger	Reflector card(s)
Monitor	Light diffusion screens
AC adaptor	External microphone(s)
Extension cord	Extra battery pack(s)
Two cassettes	Extra electrical cords
RF adaptor	Gaffer tape
75-ohm to 300-ohm adaptor	12-volt adaptor
Audio/video input cable	Remote pause switch
Audio/video output cable	Accessory lens(es)
Dubbing cables	Equipment bag or case

FIG. 7–1 A hard-shell case that protects equipment from dust and physical damage. Custom compartments hold the various pieces securely in place.

If you're shooting at home, all your supplies will be fairly close at hand. If you're going out into the field, test the equipment to be sure that everything is functioning properly. Check and double check to be sure that you have everything you need. That includes equipment, notes, storyboards, props, and so on.

SETTING AND COMPOSITION

You may not think that how a scene is composed has much to do with preparation and planning. In fact, if you don't preplan and prethink, correct composition will become a matter of chance. There's more to it than just "aim and shoot."

Preplanning may involve an in-depth survey of the area where the shooting is to take place. What is the basic layout of the area? What's there that might add to, or detract from, the scene? What will get in the way? Some quick sketches can be made to serve as reminders.

In many cases, there won't be time for this. Instead you'll find yourself "sizing up the situation" in a hurry. The process and questions are the same— you just don't have as much time. The preplan survey is a wonderful way to judge how you will approach the shooting, and how you will compose various scenes.

FIG. 7–2 Picture composition begins by setting up the scene, then checking to see what can be used, and what is to be avoided. In this particular setup, we want to get rid of the trash on the table and move the actor so the pole isn't "growing" from his head.

Framing and Closure

Framing a scene can be symmetric or nonsymmetric. A symmetric framing is balanced, and may be a scene where the subject is in the center, or one where the sides are balanced. Symmetric framing tends to be static.

Asymmetric framing is unbalanced. The main subject may be placed off to one side, or one side of the scene might contain more objects. The effect is more dramatic.

Another factor in placement of subjects in the frame is something called *closure*. In life we're used to seeing things in certain ways. If an object doesn't appear as we would expect, the mind fills in the missing details. A head-and-shoulders picture still gives you the idea that this is a whole person. Your mind fills in the detail that there is a body outside the scene. Show a tree coming in from the side, and your mind will fill in the detail of the ground, roots, and the other half of the tree.

That's closure.

FIG. 7–3 Improper closure is used in the shot at left. The subject is cut off in the wrong places, making her seem unnatural. In the photo at right, proper closure makes her seem more natural.

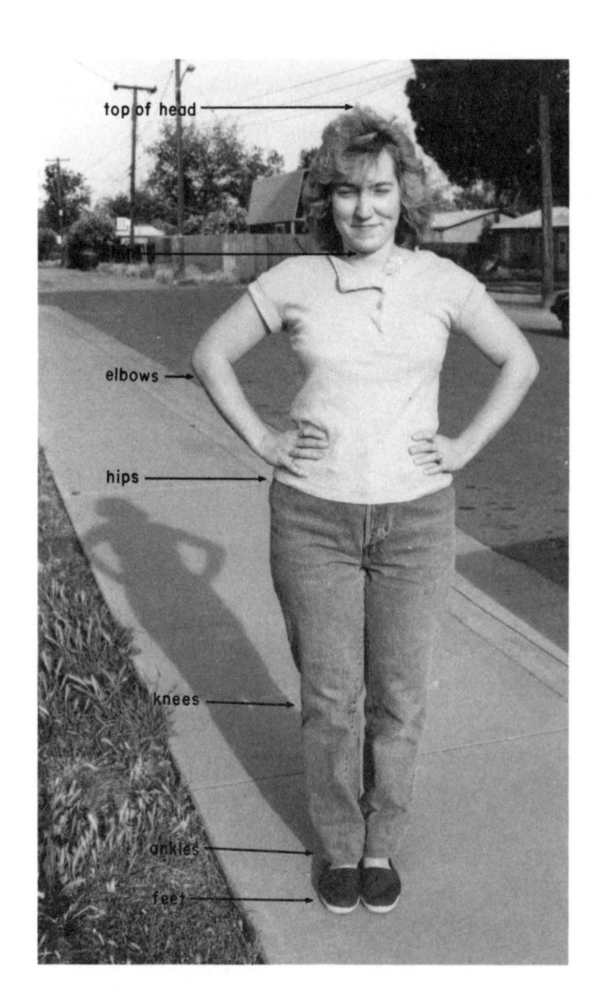

FIG. 7–4 When photographing people, take care with your cutoff lines. Shown are points where you should *not* crop.

Closure can work for you, or it can work against you. If the portion of a person or object shown is unnaturally cropped, the viewer will have more difficulty filling in the missing details.

There are natural cut-off lines, and these are especially important with people. As a general rule, they are just below the main joints and features of the body—eyes, chin, bust, elbows, waist, wrists, knees, and ankles (Fig. 7–4). Also important are clothing features, such as sleeve length or hemline. A cut-off line should never be placed at the edge of the frame. Try it and you'll see why: tape someone with the frame cutting off just the hands at the wrists, for example.

Rule of Thirds

The basic rule of rectangular composition, and even a large portion of square composition, is the Rule of Thirds. The aspect ratio of the viewfinder, pickup, and monitor screen are all the same 3:4 rectangle. Divide this into three equal parts vertically and three equal parts horizontally, creating nine smaller rectangles inside the total frame.

The Rule of Thirds is to place the subject along one of the lines. The rule also applies to stationary objects in the background (Fig. 7–5). For example, if the horizon is placed in the center of the frame, everything tends to look static. Placing the horizon either one-third up from the bottom or down from the top makes the scene more pleasing.

Merging

In outdoor shots, there are often obstructions. A tree is growing in just the wrong spot or the local utility company has planted poles and strung wires where they provide a necessary service but ruin an otherwise wonderful shot. This much is irritating. Worse is when those obstructions seem to merge with the important subjects: a telephone

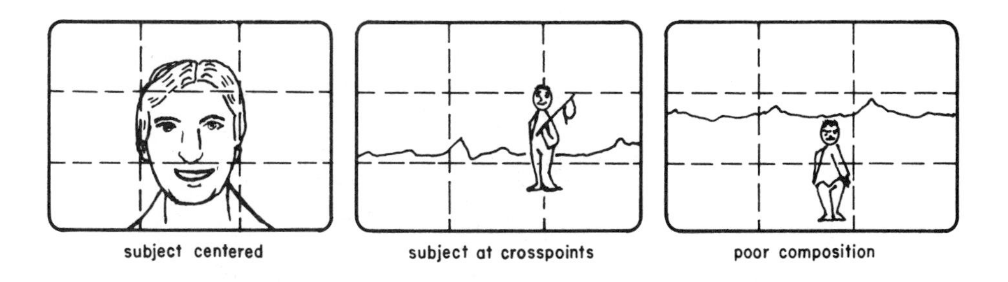

FIG. 7–5 The Rule of Thirds divides the scene into three vertical and three horizontal areas. The subject *should* be centered (left) or positioned along one of the vertical thirds (center). The horizon should be placed along one of the thirds, not in the center (right).

pole seems to be sprouting from someone's head. Or a branch seems to be growing from a shoulder.

Merging can also take place with color and even with contrast. Someone wearing a green shirt may blend into bushes in the background. A light subject will tend to disappear into a light background (and vice versa) even when the colors are different.

Low-contrast scenes have a shallower apparent depth, making it more difficult to see the differences in distance. Even in reality, it's sometimes difficult to determine distances out on a desert, on an open snow-covered field, or any place where the contrast is very low (including predominantly dark scenes). This effect is amplified by the camera and lens. With the difficulty in picking out distance and depth, merging the background with the subject can become a serious problem.

Your goal is to make sure that this doesn't happen. Look at the background to make sure that something isn't merging with the main subject. This can usually be fixed by repositioning the subject. A preshoot visit to the site can help, but constant awareness of the background plays a more important part.

To further reduce the merging effect, use the wider angle setting on the lens. The telephoto setting (zoom in) has a tendency to squash the depth, making things seem closer together than they really are. A wider angle setting will increase the sense of depth.

Controlled lighting can also help to separate the subject from the background (see Chapter 6.) Unfortunately, this is often extremely difficult to do out in the field. You're better off avoiding the situation in the first place, or using a wide-angle lens or setting to reduce the effect when it can't be prevented.

Camera Angles

Most of the time, you'll be shooting scenes from straight on, with the camera level. The design of the camera usually encourages this. However, camera angle can be used to create a variety of moods and effects (Fig. 7–6). By tilting the camera, the scene becomes unbalanced, as though it is ready to spill out of the side of the screen. Handled properly, this lends a sense of energy.

Camera height, and the angle between the camera and subject, can also change the mood. Shoot down on the subject and the subject will seem smaller and less important. The camera, and thus the viewer, will feel the dominance. On the other hand, shooting up at the subject will make the subject seem more powerful, even to the point of being ominous and threatening.

FIG. 7–6 A number of different effects can be achieved by changing the camera angle.

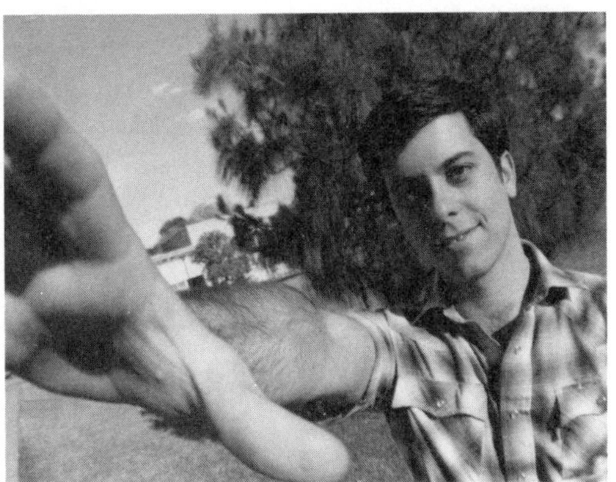

VIDEO SCRIPTING: ROUGH OR POLISHED

You can go about your shooting in a haphazard manner and settle for whatever you manage to get. Or you can make a video that is vastly superior to the "standard home movie" by determining what will be shot and in what order.

This applies to a backyard barbeque as well as to a major event. What differs is the amount of detail. That barbeque won't require a script or specific dialogue. But if you preplan at least some scenes, you'll end up with a very entertaining family home movie.

Some thought will just about guarantee it. It's not all that difficult. Just keep one simple rule in mind.

Tell a story.

A story has a beginning, a middle, and an end. There is an organization to it and a sense of order. Instead of the video hopping haphazardly from scene to scene, there is a flow.

The beginning is set with *establishing shots*, often *leading lines* guiding the eye of the viewer toward the primary scene. For that family barbeque, you could begin with shots of people walking up the driveway toward the group assembling in the yard.

The middle consists of the body of the story, in this case the events of the barbeque. Here the sequence can become more difficult to manage, since many things are happening simultaneously. One way to control your taping is to make a storyboard, sheets of notes

FIG. 7–7 A basic storyboard.

and/or sketches that includes the main events, with approximate timing and sequence (Fig. 7–7).

Later on, you can juggle scenes and edit the original recording. (You won't *necessarily* want events to appear in the order in which you shot them.) If you don't have editing equipment available, planning the sequence before the shoot becomes even more critical. Even if you have open access to the best video equipment, careful planning will make the job of editing easier.

As valuable as planning is, don't let it get in the way. The storyboard should be a servant, not a master. No matter how well you plan things, conditions may make it necessary to change. Plan ahead, but be flexible.

Continuity

Have you ever seen a movie where the character is wearing a blue shirt in one scene and a red one in the next? Or one where the camera shows a distant shot of someone driving along a road—then zooms in and the car is traveling in the opposite direction?

Both are examples of lack of continuity.

Continuity also concerns the flow. Does it move forward steadily and logically? Or does it hop from place to place?

Too many home movies lack continuity because the person behind the camera has no plan, and little idea of what to shoot and when. Instead, events are simply allowed to happen. Planning, including a storyboard, will help to create continuity. In fact, continuity is (or should be) built into the storyboard. This takes place before you begin. After you've completed the shooting, you can edit the recording to further enhance continuity.

During the shooting, there are tricks that will add to the sense of flow while also helping to make later editing easier to accomplish. The main trick is to start taping slightly before the beginning of the scene and end it slightly after the scene is over. One or two seconds is almost always sufficient. (If you *know* that you'll be editing the tape, or a particular scene, allow the lead and tail to be longer. Professionals often use 5 seconds before and after.)

For an action sequence, an easy trick is to begin taping a relatively blank scene, with the subject moving into, and then out of, the frame, followed by a moment of blank scene again. How long you "track" the subject in the scene depends on what you want.

Scripting and Dialogue

The script and dialogue for a wedding were probably preset long before you were called in. As the wedding videographer, you should have a copy of the "script" before you begin taping the wedding. It's a good idea for you to also attend—and tape!—at least one rehearsal.

Sometimes scripting plays a more important part in the production. Like a storyboard, a script gives directions and sets up a basic plan. Unlike a storyboard, a script is entirely verbal. There are no sketches or drawings. Scripts should allow some flexibility and variation. Memorized lines by amateur actors and actresses tend to sound stilted and fake. Your goal is for a natural appearance and sound. If this means adding a line here, removing a line there or ad libbing, this flexibility will probably enhance your storyline.

For most home productions, think of the script as a guideline. As with a storyboard, a script should be a servant, not the master of your recording (see sample script).

Video tape is an inexpensive and valuable practice tool for amateurs (and pros, for that matter). Your actors and actresses can do their dialogue, then watch it immediately afterward to see how improvements might be made. You *can* erase the mistakes and reuse the tape—but take a tip from the pros: keep the test tape. Those "outtakes" are often more prized by those involved than the practiced, edited, and perfected final recording.

✔ A Sample Script

(MUSIC—Toccata in D)

Open shot with title, "A Spur-of-the-Moment Production." Credit upside down, rotate upright. Pull credit through screen. Screen black.

Screen turns to starry sky as Narrator *speaks.*

NARRATOR

No one ever thought it could happen. Scientists deemed it impossible. But it will happen. Henny Penny's prediction was correct.

Switch to credit of "The Sky is Falling" on city background. (Music loud.)

Credit "Narrated by Scott Drudge" moves in from left to center. Fade to city shot. (Music softens in background as Narrator speaks.) Narrator *voice over.*

NARRATOR

Just recently, scientists have made a discovery that has caused some people in a Tempe neighborhood to leave their homes. Nobody's Comet is heading toward its final destination, here in Tempe. A theory has been developed on why this will occur. Dr. Joshua Duffalo.

Switch to shot of Duffalo. Duffalo is sitting, and speaking to the camera.

DR. DUFFALO

For approximately 5 years, my colleagues and I have been studying Nobody's Comet. This research has led us to develop a theory. Now this theory is our best to date.

Switch to graphics showing Duffalo's theory. Narrator *voice over.*

NARRATOR

According to Dr. Duffalo's theory, Nobody's Comet was bumped by a meteorite fragment that broke off the planet Reeb Fossalg. Every planet, moon and comet is rotating; due to its bumping, Nobody's Comet is not rotating properly. With each revolution, Nobody's Comet is getting closer to Earth. This is setting up a negative force on Nobody's Comet and a positive force on Earth.

DIRECTING A VIDEO PRODUCTION

At one time or another, everyone has had the experience of telling someone "Go to the left," only to have the person move to the right. When you're facing that person, your left is his right.

Professionals use specific terminology for directions. A professional storyboard and script will often contain these terms, along with symbols to represent those directions and motions. Most come from old stage productions, but the terms are used even in an open field.

The original stages were slanted so that the people in front didn't block those in the back. Consequently, as the actor walked toward the front of the stage he was walking downhill. Even after stages were built level, the words stuck. Someone "down stage" is at the front, while someone in the back is "up stage." Snagglepuss used to say, "Exit, stage left." That means that he is facing the audience and leaves to his left (the audience's right—sometimes called "house right").

Direction isn't too troublesome at home. All you have to do is point and say, "Move over there." Direction is more than just knowing terminology to show off; in most home productions, you'll be playing many roles—producer, director, writer, camera operator, editor, showing room technician, and even psychologist.

How do you get shy Aunt Daisy to demonstrate her special technique for eating raw oysters? "Move stage right and swallow" won't help. A storyboard with arrows will be of help, and might even get Daisy into position, but your job as director still isn't complete.

Candid shots are not as easy to capture as you might think. Most people are too self-conscious, unless you leave the camera on so long that everyone forgets about it. Out of a group of ten friends and relatives, you'll be lucky to find one person (over the age of 12 or without a few martinis) willing to perform for the camera. The key is *tact*, followed closely by *patience*. You'll *never* get the shots you want if you lose your temper.

Quite often, the easiest solution is to set the camera on a tripod and let it run. This will require a considerable amount of editing, but after the camera has been running awhile, with you away from it, the people being videographed will tend to ignore it.

With some acting and ingenuity on your part, you can learn to have the camera on while making it seem that it is not. This often involves sighting and framing while not looking through the viewfinder. Preplanning—knowing what the camera will be seeing while you hold it nonchalantly on your shoulder or under your arm, or have it on a table—will help. Be careful not to cross the line to sneaky, even unethical, behavior. Depending on who and what it is you're recording, judgment must be exercised. No candid shot is worth the anger of a friend or relative, much less a lawsuit!

Chapter 8

Editing: The Mark of a Pro

Without some editing, the best you can expect will be amateurish-looking "home movies." Editing is used to remove unwanted material or to juggle and blend scenes in a different order. The end result is—or should be—much more interesting to watch.

Editing can be a real chore. It can also cause glitches and image degradation through signal loss in dubbing. No matter what you do, sync lines may appear as the playback VCR tries to synchronize to the tape. Wavy "rainbows" could dance across the screen if you've placed new video on old. More serious, there is an inherent loss of signal strength with each dubbing generation. The best image and sound will be on the original. Both the video and the audio will be degraded slightly on the edited copy you make. Make a copy of this—a third generation recording—and flaws will definitely start to become apparent.

Despite these problems, and regardless of how well you plan your shooting, editing can greatly improve your movie. In fact, very few movies look professional without editing, starting with proper preshoot editing before anything is recorded at all, going through in-camera editing, "cut and paste" editing afterward, and a final edit to make sure that everything is just the way you want it.

IN-CAMERA EDITING

Editing actually begins long before you turn on the camera. Preplanning will give you an idea of what you want to record and in what order (see Chapter 7). This not only reduces the amount of editing required, but it will help to make editing easier and more successful.

The next step in editing takes place while recording: the easiest part is nothing more than using the *on/off* or *pause* button. Shutting

FIG. 8–1 The simplest means of in-camera editing is to shut off the camera, thus making a "cut."

off the camera makes a "cut," with the next scene beginning where the last left off, and with no pause or black between (Fig. 8–1). Shoot Uncle Bill by the barbeque, shut off the recording, turn to Aunt Betty by the table and start again. You've just edited out everything between by simply not recording it. You would do this naturally, all on your own, after some experience with your camera, but now you'll be conscious that you're doing it, and know why.

Taping, stopping, taping, stopping, without purpose tends to make a recording look amateurish. There are two general rules of thumb to keep in mind. First, scenes should usually be no shorter than 10 or 15 seconds, and not longer than about 5 minutes. Scenes that are too short give the recording a choppy appearance and are hard on the viewer. Longer scenes tend to be boring. The ideal is a balanced mix of longer and shorter scenes.

Remember to begin slightly before and end slightly after each scene. This gives you a visual pause, which in turn lends a smoother transition. For example, if you're trying to capture your family on a Saturday afternoon, dad might be outside mowing the lawn, while mom is digging weeds from the garden. A one-minute scene of the lawnmowing can begin by focusing on the lawn, with dad walking into the scene, a slow pan as he moves across the yard, then the camera stops moving to let dad walk out of the scene. Cut to mom in the garden for 30 seconds. The sound of the lawnmower ties the two scenes together. The flow is smooth and "natural."

Now suppose you want to achieve an unsettling effect. Sharp cut to dad. Quick cut to mom, then a few seconds later back to dad. The effect is one of building tension.

The next time you watch a good movie, pay attention to how it has been edited, where the cuts take place, and what effect it has on the viewer.

Video has an advantage that no film camera has. If you don't like what you've shot, all you have to do is to back up and shoot again. The new image and sound will replace the old. This makes it possible to do an appreciable amount of editing even as you're shooting. The

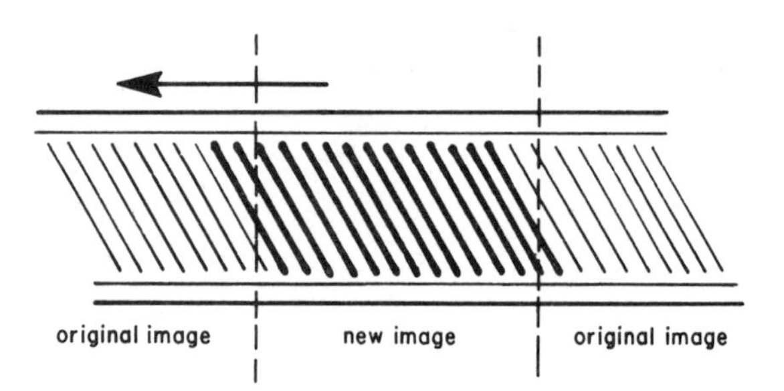

FIG. 8–2 Back up the tape and play it forward. Stop the VTR and pause, then record over the old material.

technique is simple. Back up beyond where you want to cut. As you play it forward again, pause the VTR at the spot where you want the cut to appear and switch to the record mode. Reposition the camera, and release the pause (Fig. 8–2).

With many camcorders, this is not possible. To back up, view, or pause, the camcorder must be in the VTR mode, which means that it can't record through the lens. When you switch to the camera mode, those VTR features won't work. You can still back up and view the recording, but instead of pausing you have to bring the VTR to a stop. Then you can switch to the camera mode and begin recording again. This involves a little guesswork and a bit of luck. Shutting off the play pulls the tape back out of the transport. As it loads back in, the tape is drawn through the path again. It's possible—even probable—that a slightly different spot on the tape will come into place on the recording heads.

The most serious disadvantage is that of rainbowing (Fig. 8–3). The erase head is often in a different location than the recording heads. This leaves a short length of tape where the old video signal still exists. The new video signal tries to cover this, and the result is interference between the two signals. (This effect is often minimal with a camcorder, since the parts are squeezed together more tightly than in a full-sized home deck.)

Using virgin tape will eliminate the problem, but this isn't always practical when you need to back up and eliminate a portion of a recorded scene. The solution is to use a machine with a flying erase head (see Chapter 2). The erase head is mounted on the recording

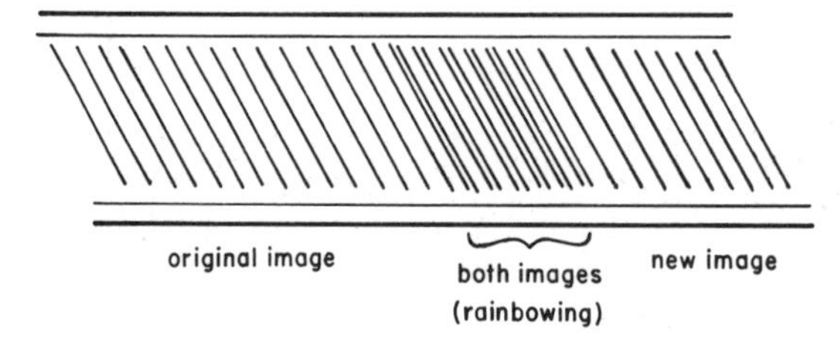

FIG. 8–3 *Rainbowing* is caused by interference when you record a new signal on a section of tape that still has the original signal.

head assembly. Erasure of the old signal takes place in the same place that the new signal comes in.

Not really in-camera editing, but still a highly useful technique, is that of recording blank. If you *know* that you'll be editing the segments into a different order, a section of blank video, such as you'd get with the lens cap over the lens, gives you a chance to pause. (The extra time before and after the scene you want, as mentioned before, can also be used to serve this purpose.) Blank video also allows you to have a "cut to black" break between scenes in the final version—an often handy device. Keep in mind that when you record with the lens cap in place, the audio is still being recorded. Either make sure that the surroundings are completely quiet or unplug the microphone.

VTR-TO-VTR EDITING

By using one VCR or the playback feature of a camcorder, and another VCR as a recording device, you can successfully edit what you've shot. With a little care and some preplanning, the end result will look quite professional.

The general method is simple. One VTR handles the playback of the tape to be edited, while the other records the new tape. Let's take a

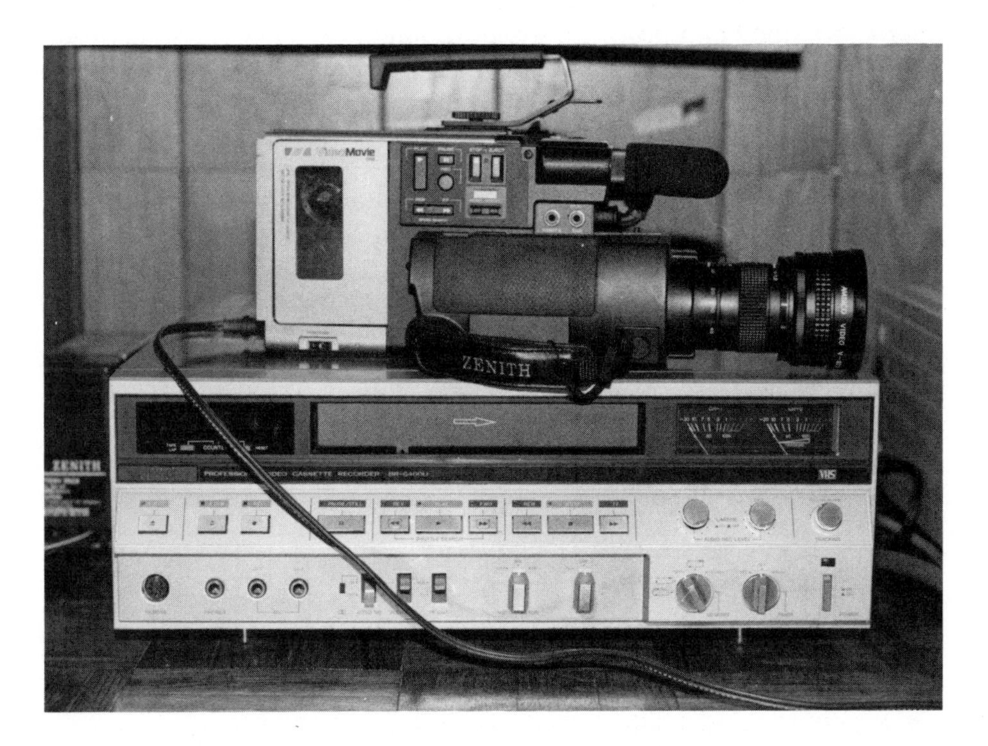

FIG. 8–4 The camcorder can be used as a playback deck.

look at one of the simplest and most common edits—removing unwanted material. If you're making a tape of yourself and the camera is on a tripod, there could be the empty room behind, then you walking in front of the camera, you leaving again, and more empty room. If all you want is the part with you in it, you'd play the entire sequence and have the second VTR record only the wanted portions.

The recording deck is set up for the proper speed and spot, then set to record mode and in pause. The playback deck is then put into motion just slightly before the wanted portion. As it reaches the part you want, release the pause on the recording deck, then pause again at the end of the scene. That's all there is to it.

You can make more complex edits using the same method and a little ingenuity. If the tape to be edited has scenes scattered out of sequence, your first task will be to preview that tape and write down the footage counter numbers for the scenes—preferably the beginning and ending numbers. By the time you're done, you'll have a complete listing of the scenes on paper, a short description of each, and the spot where they occur on the original. Now you can juggle them any way you wish. After that, it's a time-consuming matter of going to designated spots on the original in the order you want them.

If the recording deck has to be stopped, don't just start it again. Back up, play what has already been recorded, and press the pause at the end of the last scene. Then, with the pause still activated, go into the record mode and proceed as before. This extra step prevents problems. If you just start up the recording deck, you may record on top of the last important second or so of the previous scene. This could easily mean that you have to start all over again. Just as bad, you could have a small bit of tape that has nothing recorded on it. This will cause the VCR playing back the tape later on to hit a hole, after which it has to search for the cue track again. Meanwhile, the viewer will be treat-

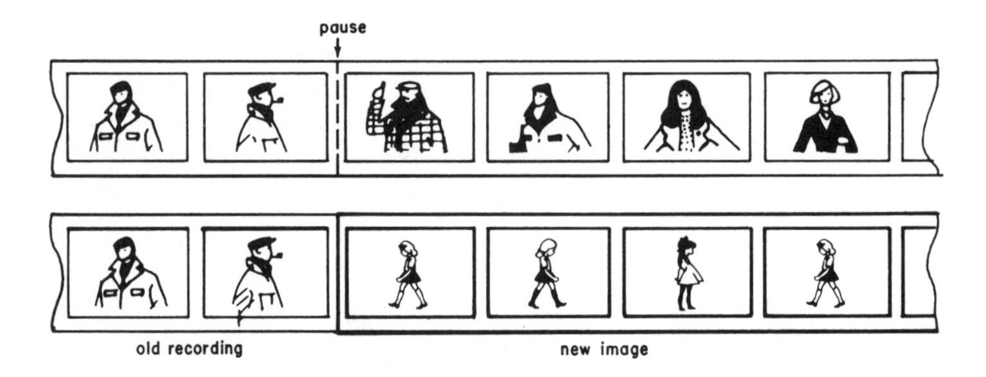

FIG. 8–5 Back up the recording deck, play what you've already recorded, then pause at the appropriate spot.

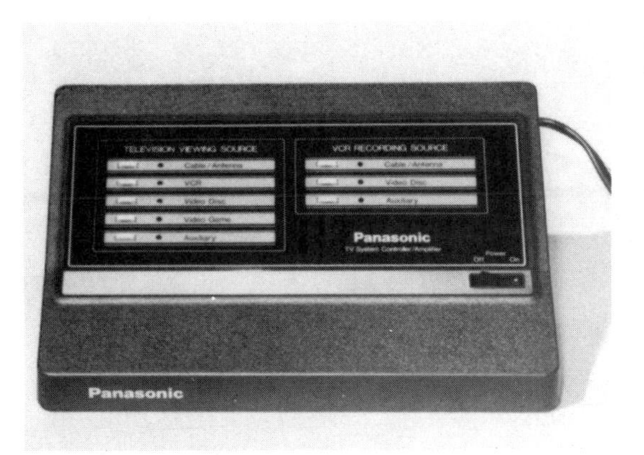

FIG. 8–6 A video switching box.

ed to a dead screen, followed by some seconds of garbage while the VCR gets itself into sync with the tape again.

You may have more than one original tape from which you want material. The problems are compounded, and even more time is needed to do the job right. As you run one tape, the numbers in the playing deck change. Put in the second original tape, and you won't know where you are. Then when you put back in the first tape, you're lost again.

The easiest way to record from two tapes is to use a VCR for recording, plus a separate VCR for *each* tape from which you want material. That way you can accurately record the footage numbers. You'll have to swap cables around as you go from deck to deck (or use a video switch box), but this is less trouble than constantly rewinding each tape to zero before going to the next scene.

Your home VCR makes up one of the needed VCRs. A camcorder can serve as a second. If you have just a camera, or have a need for a third deck, rental of the units is generally quite inexpensive. In most areas, the cost of renting a VCR for 24 hours is from $3 to $6, although many rental stores won't rent just a machine. You may have to rent at least one movie at the same time.

VIDEO EDITING MACHINES

A video editing machine is essentially a special kind of high-quality VTR. It has mechanisms and circuits for accurate control of both audio and video. Due to the cost, it's unlikely that you'll have such a machine around, or that you'll run out and buy one. Inexpensive video editors cost $2000 and up; for something that approaches professional quality, expect to pay closer to $5000.

But don't despair. With the growing popularity of home video, many larger cities have rental studios complete with all the equip-

FIG. 8–7 An editing machine is a costly, but superior, means of handling the edit job.

FIG. 8–8 A complete editing setup includes two VTRs, a controller, and a monitor.

ment. Typically, the charge runs from $20 to $35 per hour for unassisted rental, with an additional charge if one of the studio staff assists. Fortunately, operation of the machines is simple enough to understand after just a few minutes of explanation.

A professional setup is generally capable of A/B roll—meaning that two playback VTRs are being used to feed the recording VTR. This isn't as simple as it sounds. You can't just take any three VTRs, cable them together, and expect to get professional results. The machines must be synchronized. Each of the two playback decks is providing a sync pulse. A time/base corrector is needed to get the sync pulses "in step." Otherwise, when you switch from one deck to the other, the new sync pulse coming from the second deck will cause a glitch. Some complicated and expensive circuits are needed to prevent this and to coordinate the two incoming pulses.

You *can* use just two decks and swap the tapes back and forth in the playback deck. A/B roll just does the job better and faster, while allowing you to insert special effects, such as wipes and fades, between the two incoming signals and without the momentary breakup of the signal.

DUBBING

There are three major problems in any dubbing. Rainbowing has already been discussed. It is signal interference caused by two video signals on the same tape segment due to incomplete erasure of the original signal. The solution is to either use virgin tape or to use a VTR with a flying erase head.

The second major problem is the loss of synchronization. The third is signal loss.

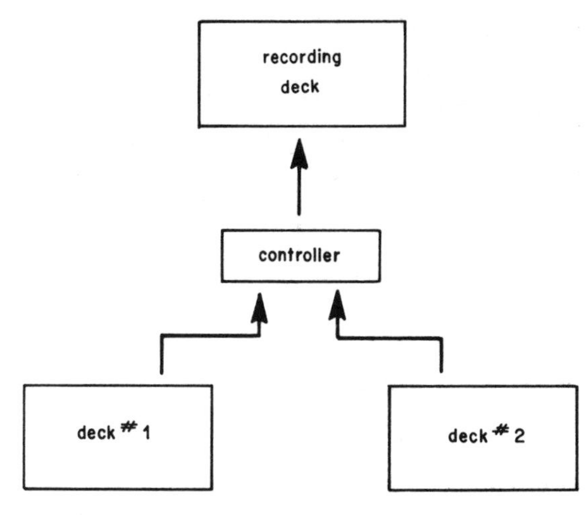

FIG. 8–9 How A/B roll works: two playback VTRs feed the recording VTR.

For a steady image from multiple sources, the separate sync pulses must be brought into step with each other. As mentioned above, this is accomplished by using a time/base corrector. In a sense, the time/base corrector forces the incoming sync pulses to be the same, as far as the recording deck is concerned. You can then switch back and forth between the two incoming signals without a temporary mixup in the sync pulses and the resultant glitches.

If you are dubbing from deck-to-deck without a time/base corrector, the effects of the glitches can be minimized by using fades or wipes (see Chapters 5 and 9). The black video will still have the glitch, but at least that glitch appears when no video is on the screen. As with anything, too much of a technique is no longer effective—it's irritating!

Signal loss is simpler. There is an inherent and general loss in the original signal strength. What happens then is that the imperfections and distortions tend to be boosted along with the wanted signal. The overall image and sound become degraded. Your goal at all times is to keep the number of generations to a minimum.

The original is the first generation. The first edited dub is the second generation. Edit and copy this one and you have a third generation. It begins with a degraded signal, which in turn means that the degradation between the second and third generations is more severe than between the first and second generations. Make a copy of that to give to relatives and you're giving them a fourth generation recording, with successive signal loss for each (Fig. 8–10). Within a short time, the signal loss is so bad that the recordings are virtually unwatchable.

It gets worse!

The less perfect the original, the more serious the degradation. For example, if the original is of poor quality due to dim lighting, the second generation (first dub) will be even worse: the green-tinged walls from the original will have a distinct greenish cast in the dub. Copy it again, and both the color and graininess could ruin the image. Go to yet another generation and the tape will be all but impossible to watch.

Successive dubs demand that the original be of nearly perfect quality. Don't expect that fancy $1000 enhancer to correct the problem. It won't. Even the best machines have to have something to work with. To build detail, the enhancer increases the high frequencies. As it does this, it also boosts video noise.

Image enhancers do have limited use, but in relatively small ways. Keep in mind at all times that they can't create an image where there is none.

Also available are signal amplifiers. One example is Ambico's "Super-Duper." This small box amplifies both the video and the audio. Their claim is that the dub is of a quality that is nearly identical to

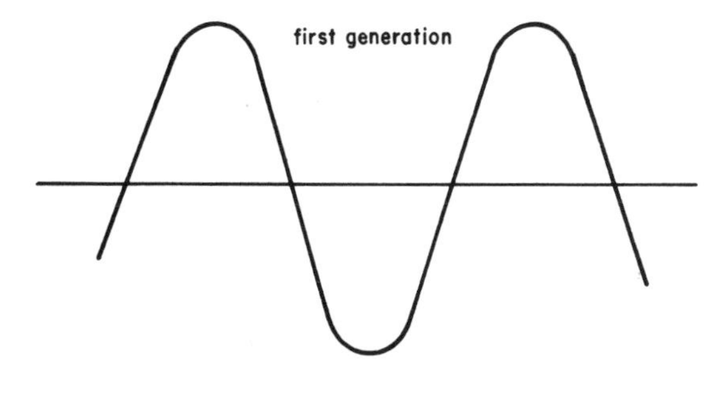

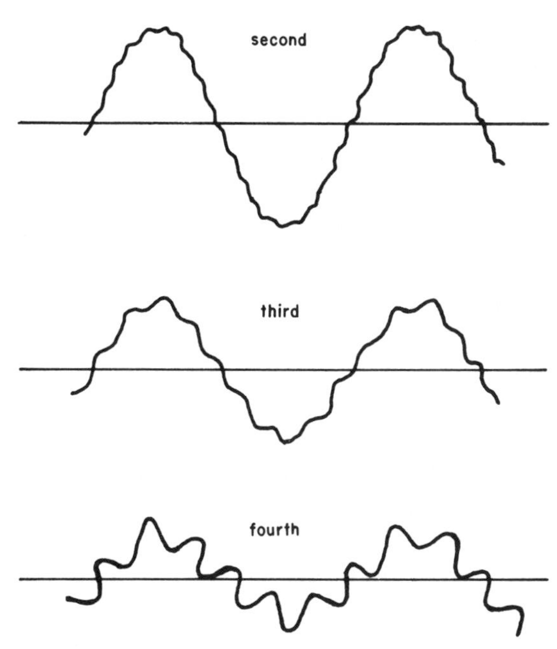

FIG. 8–10 The signal deteriorates with each successive generation.

the original. It doesn't quite meet the claim, but it *does* do a fair job and is an inexpensive means of keeping signal loss to a minimum.

Also of use is any signal amplifier that can handle both the video and the audio. A large number of these are available. The unit you use should preferably have both video and audio inputs and outputs. This makes it easier to connect the unit to your equipment. Controls for the amount of signal amplification will help in preventing overload (too much signal).

Before investing in a signal amplifier, get out the manual for the VTR you intend to use as the recording deck and see what the maximum input signal level is. In most cases, it will be 1 volt. Anything more than this will not only defeat the purpose of signal amplification (by producing distortion) but could possibly damage the machine.

Also keep in mind that all signal amplifiers are "stupid." They don't know which parts of the overall signal are wanted and which are noise. As the wanted signal is amplified, so is the noise.

Chapter 9

Creating Special Effects

Even a home movie of the family can be improved with a touch of special effects. If your goal is to make something closer to an actual movie, special effects make the difference between ordinary and spectacular.

However, you are limited by the equipment and props available to you: don't expect to produce special effects (SFX) equivalent to *Star Wars* or *Indiana Jones*. It just isn't going to happen.

Hollywood injects money. You have to inject a *lot* of imagination. That $50 million computerized stop-motion camera system with the photo-blue background is almost certainly out of your reach. It's highly unlikely that you can afford to tape an 18-wheel semi going off a cliff for that neat explosion. So, the small-time video maker must make do with whatever is available. The end results rarely look professional, but with your imagination in top gear, you can create very suitable effects while spending almost nothing.

Special effects can be divided into three general categories—mechanical, optical and electronic. Each has a purpose. Each can be as complicated, or as simple, as your budget allows. Often the three overlap.

MECHANICAL FX

Mechanical effects are achieved by doing something physical. This makes it the broadest category, including props, costumes, make-up, and even miniature models.

Some friends of mine made a fairly long video production in which the regular program was broken up by fake advertisements. At one point, an announcer comes on camera and says, "And now a word from our sponsors, Bouncy Bungie Cords from Belgium by Brennan."

The camera cuts to what looks very much like a dog bouncing by its tail from the ceiling. As the dog bounces in and out of the picture, wiggling and squirming the whole time, a voice-over says "We tied a bungie cord to this dog's tail 12 hours ago. And look! He's still bouncing."

Watching the end result on the television makes you think of calling the ASPCA. Actually, the dog was playing one of its favorite games. The simple effect was achieved by turning the camera upside-down and recording a dog jumping for a balloon, with both the balloon and the floor out of camera range.

Everything is fair game to the videographer in search of a special effect. You can find props everywhere, and then apply your imagination to adapt what you find. A classic story involves how the makers of the *Star Trek* television series ended up using salt and pepper shakers from the commissary as futuristic tools. Home and low-budget movie makers (and quite a few major studios) have done this sort of thing as long as there have been movies. Just because something happens to be a coffeepot doesn't necessarily mean that you have to use it *as* a coffeepot.

Most cities have stores where you can buy used clothing and other items. Garage and yard sales are abundant. All these are wonderful places to find unique and inexpensive costumes and small props for your movies. Many can be used as they are. Others will require some simple modification to exactly suit your needs.

You might be after a "period" setting and need some out-of-date props; in other cases, you'll need something inexpensive because it will be "used up" in your production. Secondhand clothing, for example, is often cheap enough so that it can be used for scenes where it will be ruined.

A visit to a costume shop will yield still more. Special costumes may be purchased or rented. A variety of masks are also available. More important, a fully equipped costume shop will carry various kinds of stage makeup and other supplies.

Special Costuming and Makeup

Applying stage makeup is an art. Professional makeup artists spend years learning their craft. That doesn't mean that you can't create suitable effects at home with surprisingly little effort.

Liquid latex, available from a costume shop, has a variety of uses. Applied directly to the skin, it gives the appearance of age. Used over a form, it can be used in mask making. In both cases, once it has dried it can be treated and otherwise colored, handled, or transformed. Liquid latex is one of the least expensive methods of creating dramatic, although impermanent, costuming effects. Even when "dry" it tends to be sticky. Putting powder on it (talc, for example) helps. It also has

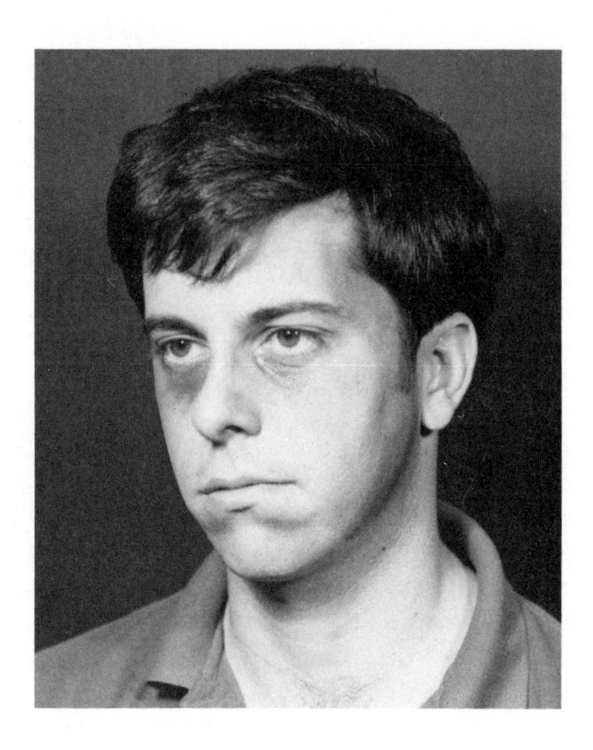

FIG. 9–1 A careful amateur can achieve credible effects with makeup.

the tendency to turn brown with age. In some cases, as with the mask in Fig. 9–2, this can actually be an advantage. In other cases you will need to paint or otherwise color the mask. Don't expect it to last forever–liquid latex is "temporary" makeup.

You can even create masks that move. The mask you create, or one that you buy, can be rigged with hinges and wires. The hinges are most often held in place using hot glue. Sometimes additional liquid latex needs to be "painted" inside to add strength to the joint. The wires can be as simple as small hobby cables pulled one at a time, or you can build more complex cables complete with hand arrays where each wire is pulled by a different finger.

Papier mâché is an effective and inexpensive way to make some masks, but is even more valuable when making larger props or sets. Chicken wire, hardware cloth, or any other suitable material can be used to make the basic form for smaller items. Larger ones may require bracing made from wood or metal. Either newspaper or paper towels can be used to make the papier mâché, the latter generally being a little lighter in weight (although more expensive).

Stage blood can be purchased, including types that are supposed to be completely washable (use disposable old clothing just in case). An excellent standby for the home moviemaker is molasses or syrup, with food coloring added. Things tend to get messy, and more than a little sticky. Clothes and other props may be ruined.

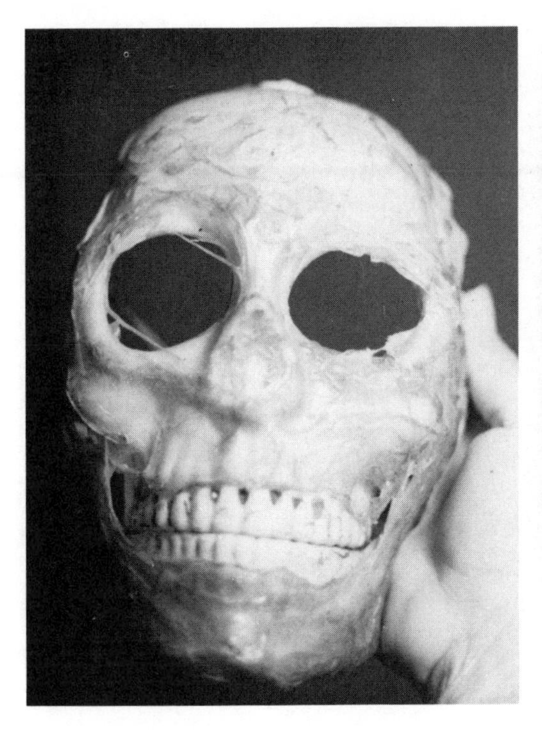

FIG. 9–2 This mask was made by spreading liquid latex over a form. The coloring in the finished mask is a natural effect of the latex aging.

Another classic home effect is to use rubber cement for spider webs. This can be done manually by dabbing the cement and pulling away fast to create the strings. More effective but more difficult to control is "spinning" the web yourself, using a cardboard form on an electric drill.

Explosions, Animation, and Other Effects

Explosions of any kind can be dangerous. In most areas, they are also illegal unless you have the proper licenses and permits. Some home moviemakers get around this by using flour and air for miniature explosions and shooting very close to the miniature. Bits of sand and other materials can also be used for realism.

There are several magazines and books on special effects. Many of these concentrate on film movies. There are certain things that can be done with film that cannot be easily done with video. Stop motion—such as for miniature modeling or animation—is one example of this: film cameras with a single-frame feature meant for stop motion are fairly common and not too expensive. The same thing is extraordinarily difficult to accomplish with video. Although the taping is being done in "frames," those frames are electronic, not physical.

Larger props and sets can be found, adapted, or even built. With

FIG. 9–3 Building a set.

some lumber, nails, paint, and time, you can build some impressive photographic sets. Combining the main set with smaller props, a complete effect can be attained. Try to save all the parts as they can often be used again. A sheet of plywood used for the floor of one set can be repainted and used as the bulkhead of a spaceship next time.

Shooting On Location

For our production, "The Ghost of Highway 12," we needed a deserted mountain road. The nearest such place that could be used safely is a 100-mile drive. Instead, we used a road running along a river bottom—the opposite extreme. Yet the trees and plants, shot from the proper angles, made the scene look more "mountainy" than even the site we originally had in mind.

You may need written permission to use a site. "Public land" doesn't necessarily mean that you can do whatever you like. An obvious example would be staging a car chase or some pyrotechnics on a public road. Less obvious are places where cameras, or even travel, are prohibited, even on government land. If you need to block a road, even temporarily, permission from authorities will be needed. If you intend to use pyrotechnics, you may need to secure a license and a permit.

We staged a gunfight for our production, "Rescue Mission," in a

FIG. 9–4 Don't forget the most available—and largest—set of all. Natural surroundings will frequently provide the best set for taping many of your scenes.

FIG. 9–5 Taping a staged gunfight, far away from other people and objects that might be damaged.

parking lot. Included was a special effect of tiny explosions on the hood of a car to simulate ricochets. The pyrotechnician had all necessary licenses and permits, the local fire marshall had been contacted, and the owners of the parking lot had granted full permission. Despite all these precautions, a nearby resident saw the gunfight and called the police. Taping had to be stopped for quite a few very tense minutes when the police came screaming into the lot from several directions with their own *real* weapons drawn.

When in doubt, contact local and state officials. Quite often a good place to start is with the local Chamber of Commerce. Many larger cities, and just about all states, have special departments set up to handle the problems and permissions of movie makers. Although they deal primarily with large movie companies, you may be surprised at the pleasant response you receive.

Shooting on private land, including a business property, *always* requires permission. This is sometimes easy to forget when the property happens to be large, such as a farm. With that great expanse available, how could the owners object to your hopping a fence and spending an hour or so with a camera in hand? *You* know that you won't do any damage. But it's still trespass and still illegal.

A professional, businesslike manner when asking for permission will go a long way. Policing the area afterward is just as important. I've found it to be a great advantage to invite the owner to watch the taping. Even after permission has been secured, don't forget to stop on the day of the actual taping to remind the owner that you are there, and perhaps to invite him again to come down to watch. Or maybe even to play one of the "extras."

Using Models and Miniatures

If you're doing a remake of a monster movie, it's a lot less expensive to have a costumed foot crunching some plastic models than it is to build a giant foot crushing full-sized automobiles. It's certainly cheaper and easier to tape a plastic satellite or spaceship against a dark sheet than to hire NASA.

Models and miniature sets are standards in the special effects industry. Nicely enough for the home video maker, quite a bit of the work of top Hollywood professionals is recreated in easy-to-assemble, inexpensive plastic model kits. You can't use them without permission for professional (or even semi-professional) productions, but they come in very handy for personal tapes.

Beyond the possible legal problems (those kits are copyrighted!), my personal objection is that they are someone else's idea. Build an X-wing fighter from a kit out of the *Star Wars* collection and you have something that is uniquely *theirs!*

An alternative to building a kit is to make your own models and

FIG. 9–6 Setting up a scene with seamless photographic backdrop.

miniature sets. You probably won't have the equipment needed to form plastic parts, but that doesn't mean you can't do a respectable job of model-making.

With the proper equipment, both wood and metal can be worked at home. Even easier is using clay or pieces of Styrofoam. A combination of materials can also be used. A main body can be made of Styrofoam, since it's easy to cut and sand. Clay can be used to fill in details. Wings can be clipped from pieces of metal.

It takes a touch of artistry to create your own models, but not as much as you might think. With some time and effort, you can create entire miniature sets. A full landscape can be built on a sheet of plywood out of plaster, sand, dirt, and a bit of paint. Miniature trees can be twigs, the stems from a bunch of grapes, or even twisted electrical wires coated with clay and paint.

Don't forget the possibility of a backdrop to complete the scene. This can be as complicated as a literal work of art or as simple as a sheet off your bed. Seamless photographic paper is an inexpensive means of providing a backdrop.

Another possibility is a structured foreground. Get a clean sheet of glass or clear plastic. Paint the foreground scene on it (keep it simple). Then shoot the main scene through that foreground sheet.

OPTICAL FX

Just about anything done to or through the lens during the taping is an optical effect. A star filter put over the lens of the camera will cause any point light sources to break into fingers of light, like a traditional impression of stars. Diffusion filters can be placed over the lens to give the scene a dreamy, cloudy effect. You can even change the color of the scene if you wish by using colored filters.

The same effects can be achieved through homemade efforts. The "star" effect can be recreated using a piece of window screen, or even a square of nylon stocking, held in front of the lens.

A diffusion filter can be recreated by using nothing more than that same nylon stocking. Plastic wrap also serves quite well for this. To increase the effect, smear some petroleum jelly smoothly over the surface of a piece of clear glass. *Never* apply the jelly to the camera lens!

Color effects can be obtained by holding pieces of photographic gel in front of the lens. Keep in mind when using any color filter that you should first adjust the camera for normal white balance and operate under manual control. Taping a scene while on auto white with a red filter in front of the lens can only cause you trouble.

Other special lighting can be used. You might want to create the illusion that the only light in a scene is from candles or from a fireplace. Or perhaps the scene involves someone reading under a lamp (Fig. 9–8). In all three cases, the amount, or direction, of light may not be sufficient for a decent recording. External light might be needed. Careful positioning will be required to be sure that the illusion in the recorded scene matches the "suggested" lighting.

FIG. 9–7 Lens accessories and filters. Photo courtesy of Ambico, Inc.

FIG. 9–8 Careful lighting gives the illusion that the light comes from the lamp, which was off when the picture was taken.

Using a special effects generator is an excellent way to create wipes, fades, and dissolves (see the next section). It's also expensive. A "down and dirty" method for a wipe can be effectively accomplished by simply pushing a piece of paper of the desired color in front of the lens. You can even cut patterns in the paper if you wish. Keep in mind that, since the paper is close to the lens, it and any cut edges will be out of focus. It's also important to remember that if the camera is set on automatic focus, a slow wipe is going to cause the main scene to go out of focus as the camera attempts to focus on the new dominant feature.

A fade is when the scene slowly dissolves into black, as though someone were dimming the lights. An easy way to do this effect is by using the manual iris control on your camera. Some cameras even have a fade feature, which automatically reduces the iris at a steady rate, causing a smoother fade.

ELECTRONIC FX

Most of what is done after taping is an electronic effect. Quite a few effects can be "built into" the original taping, but this requires

FIG. 9–9 An example of titling.

planning. If you *know* that you want to use a wipe between one scene and the next, you can use that sheet of paper in front of the lens at the right time. Or you can fade out by using the iris control. But often, you'll find yourself wanting to change what you have recorded. At this point you have one of two choices. Forget the special effect, or use a special effects generator.

Special effects generators are handy in creating a variety of effects. For example, many SFX generators can change the overall color of a scene. Another common feature is the ability to change the scene to a negative image (lightest areas become the darkest, and vice versa), often with control over the dominant color. Or you may be able to change all the darkest (or lightest) areas to a particular color, while all other colors remain true. With many units, you can also combine the controls and features.

The number of features depends on cost. Obviously, a $100 SFX generator isn't likely to have the capability or versatility of a $1000 unit. Before running out to buy such a machine, honestly evaluate your need for it. There are effects that can be accomplished *only* with an SFX generator. It's almost impossible to create a spiral wipe (where the picture is wiped off the screen a bit at a time in a spinning motion) by mechanical means. The same effect with a generator is a matter of pushing the right buttons. But do you *really* need that effect?

Another part of electronic special effects is titling. This can be done by recording pieces of paper with lettering; however, trying to create this effect mechanically is difficult and far less effective. Unfortunately, few SFX generators have character generators. Many have an

FIG. 9–10 Home equipment is unlikely to have the power or versatility of professional equipment. This studio three camera control panel is typical for a television station or professional video studio.

option that allows you to connect the unit to an external computer keyboard, which of course means that you also have to have the computer and the connecting cables.

With all that, you still won't be able to create what you see on television. A character generator might produce wonderful video lettering and numbering, but getting it to spin in and out while becoming larger and smaller—even inverting it—is often the realm of more sophisticated equipment.

A good example is a graphics generator, a step up from a character generator in that it can also generate lines, shapes, and pictures. If you want a grid pattern leading to the skyline of a city, or a map, a powerful—and expensive— graphics generator is needed.

AUDIO FX

You don't have to be satisfied with the sound already on your tape. You can replace the existing sound track. With some care, you can even blend the existing track with other audio. The simplest form is to replace the audio while dubbing. The audio output is disconnected. Feeding the audio input is the new source—perhaps an audio tape player. This *can* be done during the taping, but requires some extremely careful planning. Better to replace the audio track during dubbing.

More often, you'll want to keep the old sound track while blending in something else. Maybe a backyard scene with a thunderstorm in the distance has all the voices, but the storm is too far away to record. No problem. You can mix the existing audio track with the sounds of another thunderstorm. All you need is that other recording and an audio mixer.

Prerecorded audio is probably copyrighted (the cost of uncopyrighted material is very high). Getting a written release from the person or persons holding the copyright is often time consuming and could be impossible.

One solution is to create your own sound effects. Recording the sounds of a thunderstorm is as easy as having the proper audio equipment on hand and then waiting for the next storm. There are a number of sounds that can be gathered in the same way: screeching tires, gunshots, traffic, an angry crowd, and so on.

With a little ingenuity, you can even fake a number of sounds. Rice or sand poured onto a hard surface sounds much like rain. Crinkling cellophane in front of a microphone makes a very effective "fire." Talking into a large glass creates a hollow tone—a good imitation of someone listening in on a telephone conversation. Slap a piece of wood sharply against leather to create a very convincing gunshot.

A classic was created when "War of the Worlds" was being broadcast. The technicians and producers wanted the "unearthly" sound of a huge spacecraft door opening. A large jar top was slowly unscrewed inside a toilet, and the rest is history.

All around your home are sounds that you ordinarily ignore but which can be stored on audio tape and retrieved when needed: a refrigerator door; a creaking hinge; running water; the sound of voices in the background. Pay attention and you'll soon have an impressive "audio library" from which to draw.

SAFETY PROCEDURES

Nothing is as important as safety and there is no such thing as being too careful! This applies to using makeup and costumes, as well as doing stunts. You may be tempted to try complex costuming or stunts, which handled properly present no real danger. Handled improperly, your great video idea could quickly become a disaster.

Stage makeup is specifically formulated to be safe, but that doesn't mean 100% safe. Some people have allergic reactions. Some makeup stains the skin, sometimes permanently. Fluorinated chemical creams in particular tend to cause rashes to become permanent blotches on the skin.

More dangerous are various solvents or other chemicals used to

FIG. 9–11 Modified photographic flash bulbs were used to simulate bullets ricocheting off a car in this scene—a safe way to shoot a "deadly" script.

make or attach masks. Urethane foam, for example, is often used for making masks, and it releases cyanide gas during the curing process. Having a friend look like a monster for your movie is hardly worth wrapping a proverbial gas chamber over that friend's face.

Stunts can be even more dangerous. It's fun to watch a professional stuntman leaping off a building. But keep in mind that he *is* a professional, is wearing protective equipment, and is jumping into an air bag specifically built to protect him (inflated air mattresses aren't going to do the job), in a stunt that has been meticulously coordinated.

In short, there are a number of simple stunts you can easily pull off. But don't try to imitate the pros: it's *not* as easy as it looks. Quite often, the stunt you *think* you are seeing is nothing more than a 100% safe stunt made to look dangerous through optics and electronics.

Chapter 10

Maintenance

The first video tape machines required constant attention just to stay in operation. Like the first automobiles, tinkering was required if you wanted them to run.

Things have changed. The video equipment manufactured today is designed to require virtually no care or maintenance. Much of the equipment will even have a sticker telling the owner to stay out and that there are "No User Serviceable Parts Inside." How accurate such a sticker is depends on what the equipment is, and on you. An amplifier might have a fuse inside—a simple 25¢ "repair" you can easily do yourself. You might have enough technical background to be able to trace down simple malfunctions with a volt-ohmmeter. (See *Chilton's Guide to VCR Repair and Maintenance* for full details on what to do and how to do it.) You may even have the knowledge needed to handle more complex troubleshooting and repairs.

Or you may think of yourself as just a camera operator with no interest in repairing anything. There's nothing wrong with admitting to your own limitations, but all maintenance and even basic repairs to a home VCR are easy enough for anyone to accomplish. These steps will save you both money and time in the long run, and keep your equipment in top form.

You should *not* attempt to open a camera or camcorder to make repairs or adjustments. However, you can greatly increase the life of the unit and reduce malfunctions with some simple maintenance.

PROTECTING EQUIPMENT FROM DUST AND HEAT

The single most important way to care for your equipment is to protect it from dust and dirt. A dust cover or camera bag can help reduce the amount of dust and other contaminants. If you travel with

FIG. 10–1 One of many useful carrying cases available to protect equipment.

the equipment, it might be wise to invest in a hard case. This suitcase-like carrier not only protects the equipment from dust, it also helps to protect it from physical damage.

Something less portable, such as the home VCR, also needs protection. This begins with a suitable dust cover. Keep it in place whenever the machine isn't being used—and be sure to remove it before operating the VCR.

A second great problem is heat. Just as dust is the dire enemy of anything mechanical, heat is deadly to electronic circuits.

Anything electrical generates heat. The current flow in a camcorder is normally not high; home VCRs are more prone to heat buildup, made worse by poor operating practices, such as setting things on or closely around the VCR, so that the venting holes are blocked. The vents are there to allow the heat to escape: block them at your peril.

Another heat danger is posed by sunlight: the sun can be intense enough to melt plastic. Plastic cassette cases with plastic tape, rollers, belts, tape guides inside the VCR and camcorder, and even the plastic shells of VCRs, cameras and other equipment. Even if heat doesn't melt them, it shortens their lifespans by causing them to dry out. It

FIG. 10–2 An AC line filter.

happens sooner or later, anyway; undue heat causes it to happen faster.

Heat can also cause lubricants to break down. Add dust to that, and your delicate equipment doesn't have a chance. The simple solution is prevention. Protect your equipment to reduce the amount of dust and other contaminants that can get inside. Clean the equipment on a regular basis, and don't expose it to high heat.

SURGE PROTECTORS

Another aspect of equipment protection is keeping the incoming power clean and safe. Almost everywhere in the country, the best that a power company will provide is power within 10% of the stated value. With 117 volts nominal, this means that the actual voltage can be anything from about 105 volts to nearly 129 volts. Your local utility does not, and will not, guarantee that fluctuations in power won't cause damage to equipment in your home or business. Even if a 3,000-volt spike gets through the line and into your equipment, where it fries some delicate electronic components, with rare exception your only recourse is to pay for the repair or replacement.

The easiest solution is to buy a spike filter for anything delicate operated from a wall outlet. These devices absorb, shunt aside, or self-destruct, depending on the design, the cost, and the level of the surge. You can also get an outlet strip, a surge filter to protect the strip, and thereby protect several pieces of delicate equipment. Just keep in mind that the average home outlet can handle only 15 amps. Review the power consumption of all devices and equipment on the particular circuit. It's best to add at least 10% to the calculated consumption.

CARE AND CLEANING OF LENSES

The first thing you should do with any camera, film or video, is to invest in both a *lens cover* and a *lens protection filter*. Most home video cameras come with the first. *Use it!* Make it a habit to put the cap back over the lens whenever the camera is not in use. It takes less than a second to remove it again. Meanwhile, you've eliminated the chance of expensive accidents.

Many cameras will accept screw-on lens filters. (One of your questions when shopping for a camera should be, "Will it take filters?") Often the filter size is marked on the lens, and it will be specified in your owner's manual.

The two most common filters for protecting the lens are *skylight* and *UV-haze*. Each also has a minimal corrective effect (a skylight filter somewhat reduces the blue of shadows, while a UV-haze filter reduces haze in the distance caused by diffracted ultraviolet light), but this is much less important than protection of the lens.

Once you have the filter *use it* all the time: if you're taping a volleyball game and a small rock is kicked up and cracks the camera lens, it's a $400 accident. With a protective filter in place, it'll cost you $15. Even under the best of conditions, there are contaminants in the air that will eventually take their toll on the lens. Each time you have to clean the lens you take the chance of scratching it. With a protective filter screwed tightly into place, airborne contaminants can't get to the lens. They may ruin the filter but, once again, you face replacing an inexpensive filter instead of a very expensive lens (or having to tolerate degraded image quality).

The need to clean the camera lens is greatly reduced by using a filter; even so, you'll have to clean the lens on occasion. The first key is to use *only* top-quality material meant for cleaning the lens. Anything else can easily cause damage. Facial tissue, for example, con-

FIG. 10–3 A screw-on lens filter, such as this UV-Haze filter, is an inexpensive way to protect a lens from accidental damage and keep it clean.

tains wood fibers that eventually will scratch the lens. Ordinary glass cleaners can permanently damage the lens coating. Never use the edge of your t-shirt or a paper towel.

A proper lens cleaning kit will cost $5 to $10 and will last you for years. An excellent source is a camera store, particularly one that caters to professionals. It doesn't matter if they handle video equipment or not.

The second key is gentleness. Let the fluid do the cleaning. Don't try to scrub off deposits. If need be, clean and reclean so that the fluid can dissolve any stubborn deposits.

CLEANING VCR AND CAMCORDER INTERIORS

The most common cause of image trouble in a VCR and in a camcorder is a dirty record/play head. Remember that, to reduce the need for head cleaning, you want to use only quality tape. Protect tapes by storing and handling properly—a dirty tape transfers that dirt inside the VTR. And invest in a cover or bag—then use it!

No matter what you do, sooner or later you'll need to clean the heads. Many experts suggest that the heads be cleaned after each 20 to 40 hours of operating time, depending on the conditions. There are two ways to go about this. The easiest is to make use of a cleaning cartridge, which is like a video tape but uses a strip of cleaning material. The problem with it is twofold. First, many of the cartridges on the market tend to leave behind more contaminants than they remove. Second, even the best cleaning cartridges have a short lifespan. The first time you run the cartridge through the machine, it cleans away contaminants. Those contaminants are now trapped on the cleaning strip. The next time you use it, you're putting an already dirty cartridge into your machine. Do this too many times and you're asking for trouble.

If you use a cleaning cartridge, buy the best quality you can find and replace it often.

A much better solution is manual cleaning. In the case of a VCR, this means removing the top cover; with most camcorders, all you have to do is to push the "Eject" button, which will open the cassette door and expose the heads and other transport mechanisms.

✔ **Warning**

Never open the machine or perform any maintenance not *specifically* recommended by the manufacturer in writing while the equipment is under warranty.

The best "common" cleaning fluid for head cleaning is pure isopropyl alcohol. Specify "technical grade," with a purity of at least 95%, and preferably 98% or better. Off-the-shelf alcohol contains water, fragrance, oils, and other contaminants, which will damage delicate recording and playback heads, and other transport parts, in your VTR. *Do not use it.*

Pour a small amount of alcohol into a *clean* container and reseal the main bottle. Most people use cotton swabs, which are inexpensive and convenient. They also have a tendency to leave threads of cotton behind. Professionals suggest using *optical quality chamois*, which is clean, smooth, clear of threads, and devoid of chemicals. There are sponge pads made specially for video cleaning, but some are no more than glorified packing foam on a stick. As always, consider the heads of your VTR valuable and don't skimp on cleaning materials. Whatever you use for the cleaning, discard the material after use.

You must first have access to the inside of the VTR, which sometimes means opening the case. (Again, do *not* do this while the machine is under warranty!) For safety's sake—yours and the VTR's—shut off the power.

With a camcorder, you can generally get at everything by merely opening the door. With a home deck or portable VCR, this will involve removing the upper part of the case. With most units you need only remove two Phillips-head screws; a few will have as many as four screws. Often there is a lip on the case that tucks in, usually at the front of the machine. Don't force anything!

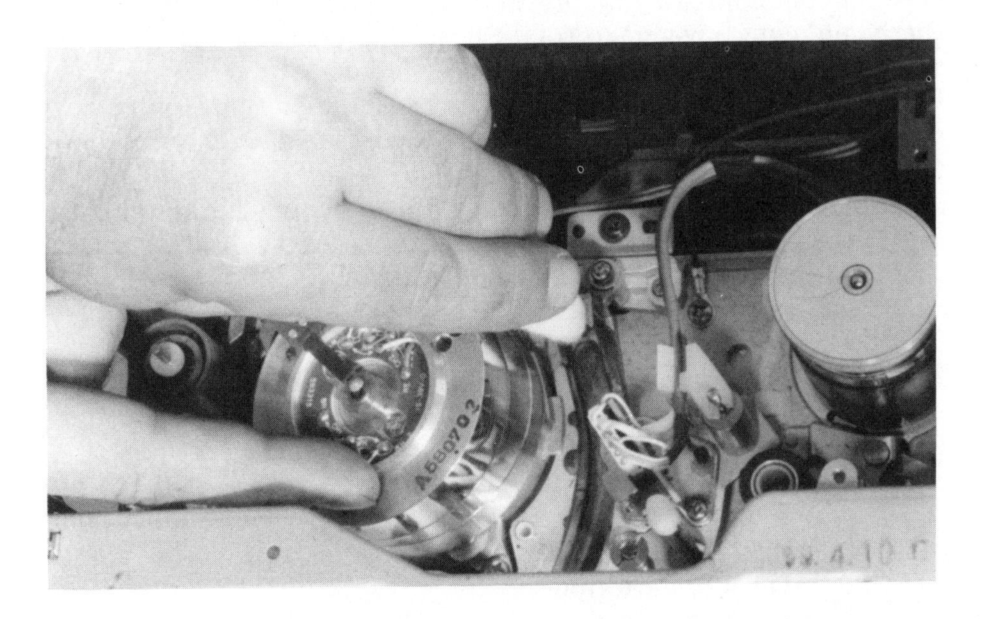

FIG. 10–4 Cleaning the heads.

FIG. 10–5 Clean other plastic parts while cleaning the heads.

Once you can get at the heads, moisten the cleaning material with alcohol. Touch it lightly against the side of the head assembly. Just as gently, put your finger on top of the head and rotate it. In other words, move the head across the pad—not the pad across the head. With a fresh pad, gently clean the audio head and the erase head, if separate—the erase head is built into the video head assembly on some units.

Next, clean all other mechanical parts, including the tape guides, capstans, and rollers. For rubber parts, you'll need a special cleaner, such as a Freon-based fluid. *Do not use alcohol on rubber!*

Visually examine the machine. Look for obvious damage, deposits of dirt, anything that doesn't look quite right. After you've been inside a few times, you'll be better able to spot potential problem areas.

Not long ago, I gave an interview on Mutual Broadcasting. A number of call-ins asked about malfunctions; in virtually every case, the solution was a simple, "Clean the machine."

Why does a VCR or camcorder "eat" a tape? Almost always the cause is a dirty machine. (If that's not it, the cause is probably either a worn idler wheel or a bad timer.)

Why does a VCR or camcorder make funny noises during recording or playback? The cause is probably dirt in the mechanisms.

Those mechanisms are essentially the same in a VCR and camcorder. The difference is primarily one of size and access.

DIAGNOSIS AND REPAIR

Troubleshooting is a process of elimination. Find out what is *not* causing the trouble and eventually you'll find what *is*. It becomes a steady string of "either-or"—either the problem is here, or it's there.

Think about the symptoms. If a tape refuses to load, but everything else seems to function perfectly, don't waste your time checking the outlet. Either the problem is with the VTR, or it's with the tape.

Now test and eliminate the easiest. Try another tape. If the second tape refuses to load properly, try a third. Now you have a pretty good idea that something is wrong with the VTR. If the second tape loads just fine, chances are pretty good that the first tape cartridge is at fault.

Professionals know that the real trick to successful diagnosis of a problem is to begin with the obvious. In the vast majority of "malfunctions," the cause is something simple and obvious. Quite often, nothing at all is wrong mechanically or electronically. Someone has kicked out the plug. Or has forgotten to remove the lens cap. Or is trying to put the cassette in backwards.

I know of more than a few cases where people have completely stripped down a VTR, only to find that the cassette had a slight warp to one edge which prevented it from loading. Instead of using the two key rules—Process of Elimination, and Begin with the Obvious—the VTR was torn apart when nothing was wrong with it.

The fine-tuned circuits and components of a camera require special equipment and knowledge. The average owner/operator can only cause additional damage by fiddling around inside the camera. What you *can* do is to eliminate all the non-problems before turning your equipment over to a professional. All you really need are your fingers and a bit of common sense, although a VOM is an indispensable tool that no home should be without.

Troubleshooting always begins with the simple and obvious, then proceeds slowly from the least complicated to the most complicated, until the cause of the trouble is found.

With a piece of equipment that is completely dead, the process of elimination begins with, "It's either in the unit, or it's not." Now you begin asking a series of questions, and performing the tests to answer those questions. If the unit is powered from a wall outlet, the test is simply to plug something else into that outlet; a breaker or fuse may have blown. It's also possible that something is wrong with the outlet itself.

If it's battery-powered equipment, such as a portable unit, chances are greatest that the batteries have run out of juice. They have an unfortunate (and expensive) tendency to fail. Those $100+ nicad battery packs can be recharged many times, but not indefinitely. Some battery-pack designs develop a "memory" for the charging cycle. In such cases, if you let the battery partially discharge to the same level again and again, then recharge, it will begin to "think" that this partially drained level is a full discharge. A battery capable of holding an hour's worth of power that is used for 10 minutes, charged, 10 minutes, charged, over and over again, then gets the idea that 10 minutes is its full capability. The solution is to at least occasionally let the battery drain completely (which can somewhat shorten the life).

If the battery won't charge at all, the "either-or" becomes *either* it's the battery, *or* it's the charger. A VOM can tell you quickly if the charger is putting out the voltage needed to charge the battery. With this eliminated, you know exactly where the problem is.

WHEN YOU HAVE TO CALL A TECHNICIAN

It's important to know your limitations. You can tackle more problems than you might think, if you proceed cautiously step-by-step. But don't go beyond your capabilities, or you can easily end up causing more damage.

If the time comes when there is no other choice but to turn your camera or camcorder over to a professional, don't do so without thinking things out carefully. Electronic equipment is becoming more and more sophisticated these days. That means it is also becoming more and more specialized. Someone trained to work on RCA camcorders, for example, may or may not be equally qualified to work on one made by Zenith. There are similarities in all makes and models. There are also some major differences. It is always better to work with only those technicians who are trained on your own specific camera.

The phone book lists shops that are qualified and authorized by particular manufacturers. If your own camera manufacturer isn't specifically listed, call around and ask. The few minutes you spend doing this can save you massive headaches later on.

There are some extraordinary repair people, and shops that have access to the needed schematics and parts for just about anything electronic you can name. Be sure to get it in writing that the shop will be fully responsible for any damage done during repair.

TROUBLESHOOTING GUIDE

Symptom	*Probable Cause*
Completely dead	Check batteries or other power source
Cassette won't load	Inserted incorrectly
Cassette won't eject	No power
No image in viewfinder	Lens cap still on No power Viewfinder unplugged
Won't record	No cassette inserted Protect tab Incorrect setting (VTR/CAM) No or low power
Won't play	Incorrect setting Connections faulty
Poor quality recording	Poor quality or damaged tape Bad connections Dirty heads
Poor quality playback	Poor quality or damaged tape Poor recording Tracking Adjust TV Dirty heads
Flagging	Damaged tape (sync track) Old TV with slower circuitry

Glossary

A-B roll: Editing and combining material from two tapes onto a single tape.

AC: Alternating current, standard in home wall outlets. An AC adaptor converts the wall current to DC so that a camera (or other device) can be operated without a battery.

AFM: Audio frequency modulation, a method of sound recording that produces a wide dynamic range.

AGC: Automatic gain control. Like an automatic volume control, these circuits are used for the video portion to keep the signal at the same level at all times.

Aperture: The opening in the lens, usually called an *iris* in video.

Aspect ratio: The ratio of height to length. This ratio is 3:4 for a standard television screen or video monitor.

Audio: Sound, recorded in a track at the top of video tape.

A/V: Audio/video.

Azimuth: The angle and alignment of the video heads to the tape.

Barn doors: Lamp flaps, usually made of metal, used to control light direction.

Barrel distortion: A wide-angle lens tends to bend lines, giving the image the appearance of looking at it through a barrel.

Beam splitter: A device used inside a camera to separate the incoming light into its primaries (red, green, and blue).

Beta: One of the two most popular video formats, developed by Sony.

Boom: A long arm, generally holding a microphone.

Camcorder: A camera and video recorder in a single unit.

Capstan: A pin, rod, or shaft, usually made of metal, that turns.

CCD: Charge-coupled device. An electronic chip used in a video camera as the video imager, instead of a tube. See also *MOS*.

Character generator: A device that electronically generates letters and numbers onto a video tape.

Chrominance: Color. The three chrominance primaries are red, green, and blue.

Color temperature: The temperature of a color measured in degrees Kelvin, determined by the amount of heat needed to cause a perfect black body to emit light. Incandescent light has a color temperature between 2700°K and 3600°K; fluorescent light, 4500°K; full sunlight, approximately 5600°K; a cloudy day, between 6000°K and 7000°K. The higher the temperature, the bluer the light; the lower the temperature, the redder the light.

Cometing: The red or blue streaks that tail a bright object when either the camera or that object moves. Common with tube cameras. Also called *comet-tailing.*

Common: The ground of a circuit, or the common path by which electrons return to the source, thus making a complete circuit.

Contrast: The comparison of the brightest areas to the darkest.

Control track: The track at the bottom of the tape on which the sync and cue signals are recorded. Also called the *cue track* or the *sync track.*

CRT: Cathode ray tube. Used as a picture tube in a television set.

DC: Direct current, such as from a battery.

Depth-of-field: The range of focus at a given lens opening. The wider the opening, the narrower the depth-of-field (the smaller the range at which the subject is in focus).

Dew sensor: A device or circuit that automatically signals the operator and/or shuts down the camera or VTR when the level of moisture is potentially damaging.

Dichroic filter: A mirrorlike device that can separate white light into the primaries (red, green, and blue).

Diffusion filter: A device, usually attached to the front of the lens, to give the scene a soft-focused (slightly out-of-focus) appearance.

Dropouts: Holes in the image, literally. Caused by pieces of the magnetic media flaking off the tape, or by contaminants on the tape.

Dub: To transfer the image and sound from one tape to another.

E/V: Electronic viewfinder. Like a miniature television set, it displays to the camera operator what will be recorded. Most video cameras use an E/V rather than an optical viewfinder.

Flagging: A bending of the image at the top and/or bottom of the monitor screen. Also called *hooking.*

Flutter: Audio distortion, primarily in the higher frequencies.

Foot-candle: A measurement of light intensity. The amount of light given by a standard candle at a distance of one foot.

Foot lambert: A unit of measurement of luminosity or brightness. One foot lambert is equal to $1/\pi$ foot-candles per square foot.

Frame: A single picture image. There are 30 frames per second in video, with each frame made up of two fields.

f-stop: The measure of the opening (aperture) of a lens. The smaller the number, the larger the opening and the more light going through the lens. Also, the wider the opening, the smaller the depth-of-field.

FX: Special effects. Sometimes abbreviated *SFX.*

Genlock: To synchronize two or more sources, particularly cameras feeding a VTR deck.

Ghost: An image echo, usually caused by either a reflection of the original signal or by some kind of signal lag.

Glitch: Interference, often caused by low frequencies. Sometimes used to describe an error in the recording and/or reproduction.

Ground: See *common.*

Head: Any of the electromagnetic devices that record, read, or erase video and/or audio signals.

Helical: The diagonal placement of video signals on the tape, due to the spiral-like path of the tape over the video heads.

High-Z: High impedance.

HQ: High quality. A special circuit, or circuits, designed to produce a higher quality image. The three basic types of HQ circuits are white-clip, luminance noise reduction, and chrominance noise reduction.

IC: Integrated circuit.

Image lag: When a bright image continues after the camera has moved away from it, causing a streak. Also called *tracers*.

Impedance: Unit of AC resistance. For proper operation of an amplifier, the input impedance must match that of the amplifier.

Incident light: Light that strikes the object directly, as opposed to reflected light.

Iris: The opening of the lens. Also called *aperture*.

Lag: A "tracer" or smear of light behind a moving object (or an object being photographed while the camera moves). Especially common in low-light conditions photographed by a tube camera.

LCD: Liquid crystal display.

LED: Light emitting diode.

Low-Z: Low impedance.

Luminance: Brightness.

Lux: Measurement of light sensitivity. The lower the number, the more sensitive the camera. The word comes from the combination of the words "lumen" and "flux" and is the metric measurement of a meter-candle.

Macro: A lens capable of extreme closeups.

ME: Metal evaporated. A newly developed method for the manufacture of 8mm video tape. Metal is condensed onto the tape by use of a vacuum, instead of being deposited and bound. Not presently in use.

M-loading: Describes the basic shape of the loading pattern of VHS.

Monitor: Like a television set, often without a tuner and sometimes of higher than usual quality.

Moiré effect: Interference, such as when narrow contrasting stripes cause interference with the scanning of the camera and/or the monitor.

MOS: Metal-oxide-semiconductor. An electronic device that draws very little current, thus allowing longer battery life. Also used as a pickup device.

MP: Metal particle. Used in 8mm video tape manufacturing.

Neutral density filter: Reduces the amount of incoming light (for example, when the light on a scene is too bright) without changing any of the colors.

Newvicon: One of the two most common pickup devices used in home video cameras.

Nicad: Nickel-cadmium. A type of rechargeable battery.

Noise: Distortion. Unwanted signals in audio or video.

ohm: Unit of electrical resistance. Also the unit of measure for AC impedance.

PCM: Pulse code modulation. The method used in 8mm video for stereo.

PET: Polyethylene terephthalate. The technical and generic name for Mylar, the plastic base used for recording tape.

Pickup device: In the camera, translates light into electrical signals that can be processed and stored on tape. Also used to describe a microphone or any device that "picks up" a signal.

Pixel: Picture element. One of the tiny light-sensitive spots on the CCD or monitor.

Rainbow effect: A term to describe the colored lines that wiggle across the screen when a new video signal is placed over another that was not completely erased.

Resolution: The clarity of the picture, measured in the number of vertical and/or horizontal lines and/or pixels used by the camera imager or the monitor screen. The higher the number, the better the resolution.

RF: Radio frequency. RF adaptors (also called converters or modulators) are used to make it possible to display the video and audio signals through a television set.

Saticon: One of the two most common pickup devices used in home video cameras.

Scanning: The process of breaking a complete image into parts which can then be stored electronically or magnetically; or the reverse process, in which recorded signals are translated back into audio and video. A television uses 525 scanning lines to make a picture.

SEG: Special effects generator.

Shotgun microphone: A highly directional microphone, used to pick up audio at a distance.

Skewing: The angled motion of the tape. Also describes the time gap between two signals.

S/N: Signal-to-noise ratio. The comparison of wanted signal to unwanted signal.

Sync: Synchronizing signals, recorded at the bottom of the tape. These recorded pulses tell the VCR where to start, what speed to use, and other operating information. Sync pulses are also used to keep two or more devices operating in step.

THD: Total harmonic distortion.

Time/base corrector: Device used to coordinate the video signals from two sources.

Tracking: An adjustment that allows the tape to move across the heads in a specific manner. This allows for minor adjustments for optimum playback with tapes from other VTRs.

U-loading: Describes the basic pattern of the tape loading of Beta.

UHF: Ultrahigh frequency, in the range of 300 to 3000 MHz. Television channels 14 and above are in the UHF band.

VCR: Video cassette recorder.

VHF: Very high frequency, in the range of 30 to 300 MHz. Television channels 2 through 13 are VHF.

VHS: One of the two most popular video formats, stands for Video Home System. Developed by JVC (Victor Company of Japan, Limited).

VHS-C: A small cartridge using the VHS format.

Vidicon: Generic term used to describe a video pickup tube.

VIR: Vertical interval reference. A system used by some television sets for automatic hue control, which can cause problems when playing encoded tapes on a television set that has VIR. The VIR may also make some regular tapes play back too bright, too dim, or with other problems.

VTR: Video tape recorder.

White balance: White is the correct blending of the video primaries of red, blue, and green. The white balance control sets the colors of the camera.

Index